# SCALE MODEL
# AIRPLANES

**Other titles in this series include:**

# Scale
# Model Airplanes

David Boddington

ARGUS BOOKS

**Argus Books**
Argus House
Boundary Way
Hemel Hempstead
Hertfordshire HP2 7ST
England

First published by Argus Books 1990

ISBN 1 85486 019 4

Phototypesetting by GCS, Leighton Buzzard
Printed and bound in Great Britain by
William Clowes Ltd, Beccles

# Contents

Dedication
This book is dedicated to Ismael, Vincente, Daniel, Paco, Mariano
and all the staff at Ses Figueres Hotel, Talamanca for making my
working break in Ibiza so comfortable.

# Chapter 1
# Where to start

THIS CHAPTER might equally be entitled 'Where not to start', as there are many enthusiasts about to enter into areas of the hobby that should be left until they are at a more proficient stage. Building and flying scale models should be a natural progression from the stages of learning to fly with training models and advancing to more challenging sports designs. It is not impossible to learn to fly with a true scale design, but there will inevitably be accidents during this phase and scale designs are more complex to build and difficult to repair. Some of the simple scale designs, such as the Piper Cubs and Cessna high wing types, are nearly as easy to fly as a purpose-designed trainer, while others are considerably harder to fly and require a fairly high degree of competence. For those of you about to embark on this exciting and rewarding hobby of radio control model aeroplanes may I steer you first towards the essential learning stages which, I can assure you, have their own challenges and satisfactions.

The companion books to this Radio Control Handbook are a series of titles including *Building from plans, Operating R/C engines* and *Installing R/C Aircraft equipment* or, for a more comprehensive publication, my *Building and Flying Radio Control Model Aircraft* (all published by Argus Books) which deals with most aspects of building and learning to fly. Reading these titles will put you on the right path to success and prepare you for the delights and challenges of scale modelling.

On the other hand, if you are already past the tyro stage, I hope this handbook will help you to consider the potential, the possibilities and how to avoid—or overcome—some of the problems of scale modelling.

To many modellers, making and flying scale miniature replicas represents the pinnacle of their achievements. The necessary process of learning to build, finish and fly a model has been a means to an end, the end being to fly a scale representation of a full-size prototype. Some critics of our hobby assume that we are following in this path because we do not have the facilities to fly *real* aeroplanes. This is quite untrue, and I know of many enthusiasts who indulge in both full-size flying and R/C modelling with equal pleasure and satisfaction. Ours is not a substitute hobby—it is a creative form in its own right. Just think of some of the skills it incorporates—designing, draughting, woodworking, metalwork, artistic demands (including those of the forger and faker!), not to mention the additional demands of flying our creations.

Because we are building accurate

7

replicas of existing aircraft (although some examples may only be replicas in a museum, or of a genre rather than a specific aeroplane), we need to get to know the full-size article. Inspecting aeroplanes, watching them fly, getting the 'feel' of the various types and generally learning how they operate is an important part of being able to recreate them. You may not be able to watch the precise example of your chosen subject in the air but, if you attend Air Displays or Flying Days, you should be able to watch a variety of types flying. These will range from the earliest types, ie. Bleriots, through WW1 and WW2 aeroplanes, representatives of historic light aircraft and on to modern jets. Absorb as much as you possibly can of the 'atmosphere' of these aeroplanes, as well as the more obvious detailing and colouring. For a scale model to look truly authentic in the air, it is not sufficient just to have the correct proportions, outlines and colours. The best examples have that little extra which gives the model 'believability'; a word not easy to define but which depends on creating the atmosphere of the prototype and on understanding the original.

Before starting to build any specific scale model, you should make an honest appraisal of your abilities as a designer, builder and flier. If you have never designed an R/C model aircraft of any type, then you should not be contemplating a scale subject as your first attempt. As an initial attempt, have a go at a sports or semi-scale project first, possibly redesigning a known sports model to look more scale. When you have made a success of this, you can progress to the simpler examples of scale subjects.

Decide whether you are going to opt for a 'super scale' standard or the less demanding 'sports scale'. Take your

flying ability into consideration at this stage. Frustration lies ahead if you build a superb, highly detailed scale replica and then crash it on your first flight. Be honest with yourself, take your entry into scale modelling at a steady level and you will be rewarded with success and satisfaction. By all means be ambitious and aim high, but reach these heights gradually.

Never forget that our principal aim is to produce a scale model which will fly. This is what differentiates our particular hobby from 'solid' scale modellers, where the models may be fabulous replicas but are destined to remain forever earthbound. Better that we have a very 'sports scale' model performing well in the air than a highly detailed model where the builder is frightened to attempt to fly it—known in the hobby as a 'Hangar Queen' (the model, not the pilot!).

Not all wish to go to the limits of designing their own scale models and some believe that this is beyond their capabilities, but this is rarely the case. With a little bit of experience and a minimum of draughting skills, it is surprising what can be done. If you decide to build from a plan, you will find that there is a wide range of scale subjects and sizes, particularly if you include the designs available from abroad. Kit designs are obviously a little more limited. The manufacturer has to think in terms of volume sales and tends to keep to the popular prototypes which he knows will have a good sales potential. Even more limiting are the ARTF (Almost Ready To Fly) assembly kits. These represent a large investment to reach a marketable stage and manufacturers can only introduce new designs occasionally. Scale fidelity will also vary from one example to another (this applies to plans, kits and ARTF models) and, if you are a scale accuracy

**High wing monoplanes, of the Piper Cub, Cessna and Auster types, make an excellent introduction to scale R/C flying. The Christen 'Husky', above, is a natural successor to the ubiquitous 'Cub'.**

fanatic, you will probably be better advised to do your own thing. At least if it is wrong, you will only have yourself to blame.

Research is another factor in the equation leading to the right scale answer for you. For many scale modellers, one of the most interesting and exciting phases of producing the replica is in choosing the subject and then carrying out the research to the stage of providing sufficient information to produce an exact replica. For competition scale modellers, this is not only a pleasant task but a necessary one, as the information must be presented in documented form as part of the static judging requirements. Not that we will all want to enter scale competitions as, for many, the satisfaction will come on a more individual basis and the most important praise will come from a fellow pilot who 'thinks it looks exactly like the full-size aeroplane'.

My aim in this Handbook is to create the enthusiasm and to start you on your way towards a successful and profitable participation in this branch of the hobby. It will not be possible to give you all the answers to specific questions but I hope there will be sufficient information to be able to find the answers, or work them out for yourself. This Handbook is limited to prototypes of powered, fixed wing aeroplanes; sailplanes and helicopters are dealt with under separate Handbook titles. One thing is for sure, you will never run out of prototypes to model. If you took every aeroplane built and flown over the past century (and some that didn't fly, but might do so as an R/C model) and put them nose to tail, they would stretch a very long way!

Increased wing dihedral on the 'Cub' makes the model even easier to fly.

Biplanes are generally easy to fly, but more difficult to build – and repair.

Low wing models, such as the Ryan STA above, should only be considered after you have served an apprenticeship with aerobatic sports models.

# Chapter 2
# Selecting and sizing

IN THE early days of R/C scale model-ling, when radio equipment was non-proportional and less sophisticated, there were a number of taboo subjects which were generally considered as 'impossible' to fly. Among these prototypes were examples such as the Westland 'Lysander', De Havilland 'Comet' (the twin engined racer) the F-104 'Starfighter' and many others that were put on the 'disasters waiting to happen' list. It speaks well of the improvements of radio control equip-ment—plus the introduction of gyros, multi-engine automatic speed controls and other electronic aids—that all of these subjects have now been built and successfully flown.

One other contribution to the success

Look at those tapered wing tip profiles! A recipe for disaster unless great care is taken with design and flying.

If you want to fly scale models of 'difficult' prototypes then build as large as possible. The author designed this DH 'Comet' to quarter scale; with two Zenoah 23cc engines (and judicial use of wash-out) it performs beautifully.

of flying previously-considered difficult prototypes often goes unnoticed. Over the years, model engine development has allowed larger capacity and more powerful motors to become available to all modellers. Allied to the greater reliability of radio outfits, the introduction of larger output servos and specialised linkages and accessories, it has become possible to build and fly safely larger models. Many prototypes which would be a 'real handful' in small scale sizes become relatively docile and reliably controllable when increased in size. This is especially true for multi-engined models, and for designs with small wing areas compared with the bulk of the fuselage. Building larger makes it much easier to reduce the wing loadings as weights of the radio equipment—or engine capacity and power—do not increase in proportion to the model size. There are other factors, including aerodynamic efficiency, which favour large scale models.

Having said that most subjects are now capable of being modelled and flown, it doesn't mean that some types are not more difficult than others. There are many factors to take into consideration. If our flying abilities are only modest, we should be looking for a prototype with a certain amount of inherent stability. The high wing monoplanes (particularly if they have some dihedral) will have this, and so will some of the well proportioned (in model terms) biplanes of earlier days. For those of you competent in flying aileron-equipped sports models, then you can progress to a further range of low wing prototypes of the trainer or sports flying type. For the competent R/C flier with experience of a whole range of models, including fast aerobatic types, then the choice of prototype is much less limited. Just leave the multi-engined and 'odd-ball' designs until you have one or two conventional scale models under your belt.

Practical considerations in your selection of the model will include size (for transportation, building and storage), the engine sizes you have, or are prepared to buy, and the radio equipment to be used. Building and flying scale models does not presume the latest in computerised R/C equipment

Certain scale models – with inherent stability – can be flown with two-channel R/C equipment. This Sopwith 'Swallow' is lightly constructed and uses only rudder and engine throttle control.

with all the bells, whistles, knobs and switches so often part of these hi-tech outfits. You can have great fun flying scale models with only two functions (rudder and engine control), although your choice of prototype is obviously more limited to relatively stable designs. Naturally, if you wish to model a prototype and include retracting under-carriage, flaps and other systems, in addition to the basic four controls of rudder, elevator, ailerons and engine, then you must have the radio equipment to cope with these functions.

Where you fly your models will also dictate the choice of prototype, to some degree. For instance, if you fly from a small grass strip—albeit a close mown one—you can forget fast flying models with retracting undercarriages. Such a model will take quite a long take-off run, and an equivalent landing distance, and you will be into the rough grass before you are safely airborne. For these flying sites (and they represent the majority of model club locations—few have hard standing runway facilities), a slower flying, more lightly wing loaded subject would be more appropriate. Do you really like building a highly complex and detailed model? If not, choose a more

Early German 'Doppledecker' will give plenty of challenges for the enthusiast of scale detail.

simple project which can be built in a relatively short time. This way you will not become bored and abandon the model half built.

Having got rid of some of the more basic and practical considerations (who mentioned money?), we can now move on to the really mind-blowing choice of prototypes ranging from the slow flying, hardly-got-off-the-ground, earliest ex-amples of manned flight, to the latest, hypersonic jet aircraft. Ironically, some of the hardest scale models to fly in a realistic manner are the early aeroplane scale replicas. The prototypes were only just capable of flight and had a speed range of only about 15kph, ie. from a stalling speed of, say, 55kph to a top speed of 70kph. This calls for some fairly delicate scale model flying, as I found out during the filming of a television series featuring R/C models of this vintage. Equally difficult are modern jets which use all types of lift-enhancing devices (leading edge slots, extending wing flaps and boundary layer blowers) to reduce the take-off and landing speeds to something manageable. In model terms, this still represents a terrifyingly high scale speed, even if we have the advantage of replicated lift-enhancing devices.

Between these extremes we have a host of aeroplane prototypes which should satisfy all scale palates. Ignoring sailplanes, we have two basic types of powered aeroplanes—piston engined and gas turbine. Yes, there were a few rocket powered aircraft and there are prop/turbine engines, but the latter can, in modelling terms, be considered as prop-driven types.

Let us consider the 'jet' prototypes first, as these present more modelling limitations than the prop-driven aero-planes. We can rule out the use of model gas turbine engine as a power source for our scale projects. You can probably count on the fingers of one hand the number of prototype model gas turbine engines that have been successfully run, and there is no sign at present of them being put into serious commercial production. Pulse jet motors have been with us for over forty years (they were first fitted into control line models) but they are pretty crude, noisy motors which have the further disadvantage of being essential one-speed devices, ie. flat out or flame out, and tremendous heat generators. The rear thrust tube can be seen glowing red hot! For all these reasons—as well as the fire risks of a model going astray—the use of a pulse jet motor in a scale model cannot be advised.

This leaves us with one option for simulating a 'jet' powered aeroplane, without resorting to fitting a conventional propeller at the front or rear of the model (often done and quite acceptable for sports scale flying, but not, of course, suitable for contest scale models). A ducted fan unit is basically a multi-bladed fan fitted to a powerful engine and enclosed in a shroud. The unit is fitted into the fuselage, or engine pod, with suitably sized air inlets and outlet ducts connected. Not quite as efficient

Eleven feet wing span Boeing 767, designed by the author, uses two spark ignition engines with propellers in place of a 'jet' engine.

as an external propeller arrangement, and certainly more difficult to install and operate, the DF units have certainly improved over the years and are now providing the performance· to recreate jet flying with R/C models. Gone are the days when, because of the poor power to weight and size performance, the scale jet was a travesty of the prototype's flying performance. Now the BAC 'Concorde', the 'F-20' and the 'Starfighter' have all been made to

Ducted fan units are used on this radio controlled Me 262.

perform convincingly. What do remain limiting factors on the selection of gas turbine powered prototypes are the inlet and outlet duct sizes. The model DF units require certain minimum areas and these *must* be adhered to for adequate thrust achievement. You can 'cheat' by enlarging the true scale inlet and outlet sizes or, as is often done,

Modern jet airliners are not often modelled – miniature gas turbine engines are not readily available.

make a false intake hole in the underside of the fuselage. It remains vital, however, to keep to the minimum areas recommended by the manufacturers of the units. Increased capacities and power of the DF engines (whereas a '40' engine was standard a few years ago, the specially designed '90' powerhouses are regularly used now) have gone a long way to producing the performance required for simulating high speed prototypes.

For piston engined (propeller) prototypes, the sky is literally the limit. There are so many options available that it is impossible to enumerate all their advantages and disadvantages. It really does come down to individual choice, allied to your own limitations of building and flying. As I have said before, there are 'naturals' for R/C scale work where the proportions are similar to the designs we would produce when scale realism was not a factor. A look at the three-view of a particular prototype should give a good indication of its potential model flying capabilities and of the complexity (or otherwise) of construction. For an easy flying model, we should be looking for a prototype with a generous wing area (with a wing plan form with a parallel chord or only slightly tapered) long moment arm to the tailsurfaces (also of generous areas). The nose should be fairly long, so that we do not finish up with consistently tail-heavy models and the fuselage design should be a 'rounded off box' for ease of construction. From these basic parameters you can develop into whatever complexities and challenges you wish.

Because the overriding consideration must be to attain a scale-like effect, a major consideration must be to attain a scale flying speed. There have been numerous arguments regarding scale speeds. Some argue that it *is* directly related to the linear scale of the model, ie. a one-fifth scale model should fly at one-fifth of the speed range of the prototype. Others calculate the model flying speed as the square root of the original and some claim that there is no absolute scale relationship but a subjective 'eyeballing' of the model (after all, a full size 'Jumbo' looks as though it is flying *too slow* to stay in the sky). However, there is no doubt that small scale models nearly all fly at faster than scale speeds, and it is only when we get into the larger scales (say one-fifth scale and above) that we are approaching true scale speeds.

Modern movements towards larger models have undoubtedly been influenced by the better flying qualities of these 'miniature aircraft'—some are almost too large to be termed models. It certainly increases the scope of prototype choice. Where this 'big is better' movement will end is anyone's guess—there have even been rumours of a 1.1/8 (112.5%) sized R/C Jodel being built!

Fortunately, we do not all have to build larger models and there is much fun and enjoyment to be had from building and flying all types of scale models (indoor scale R/C—electric power—is one of the latest innovations). The choice is wide and yours for the selection.

**Mega model! 425cc engine, three radio systems. Only for the very experienced.**

# Chapter 3
# Information sources

**Top-scoring DH9A by Peter McDermott, who had access to works drawings and photographs for his 'museum quality' model.**

HOW MUCH information you need, and how much research you will have to undertake, will depend on the scale standard of the model. If your aim is to build to FAI contest qualities, ie. super scale with full detailing, then you would be better off with the prototype available for inspection. Regardless of how many photographs may be available or how detailed the scale drawings are, you will almost certainly reach a stage of design or construction where some important piece of detail is missing, or not entirely obvious. Having said this, it must be admitted that the top scoring scale R/C static model in the last World Championships (and European Championships) was Pete McDermott's DH9A which was built from works drawings and photographs. However, the quality of photographs and quantity of accurate manufacturing drawings were exceptional. There is no need to emphasise the advantages of having the actual prototype close at hand for inspection. The only time it can be detrimental is when the intention is to produce a sports scale model—the amount of detail on hand can then cloud the issue.

Where no prototype exists, we must at least be sure, for high class scale modelling, that there are available, accurate drawings and clear photographs and reliable information on colour schemes. Obviously this limits prototype selection to some degree, but not excessively. There are directories published listing extant aircraft, private-ly owned and ones kept in museums, both on public view and in store, and it is surprising just how many actual examples are retained in the world. So, before you assume that no example exists, do check all possible avenues to ensure that this is actually the situation. Even if you cannot visit a particular prototype, you may be able to get special photographs and information from the owner or curator of the museum.

Even when there is a surviving example of the prototype you are going to model, you will still need the basic information of scale drawings, unless you are able to undertake the full measuring of the aeroplane yourself. This is quite a task and should not be undertaken lightly. Commercially-produced scale drawings vary enormously in accuracy standards, and it is not possible to give absolute answers regarding particular publishers who have the most accurate drawings. For instance, many of the ASP scale drawings are excellent, but not all of them can be considered as faultless—the same applies to the Japanese Koku-Fan publications, although these also include colour spreads and many excellent photographs (this can be done when the subjects are mainly from the WW2 period to the present day). Keeping to a particular author of drawings can be one method of guaranteeing quality standards. The names of Bentley and Lloyd spring immediately to mind. Unfortunately, some well known names do not ensure the same standards of excellence. One popular American aviation draughtsman would appear to have completed the drawing and *then* scaled it to arrive at the dimensions to a 1/4inch.

Obviously, for sports scale there is no demand to be accurate to the last inch or so, as the importance lies in the overall effect of the model. Does it look a convincing representation of the prototype? Do the hard surfaces, ie. metal, look hard and the fabric-covered areas look right? One kit manufacturer produced a series of designs under the title of 'Character Scale'—it was a good term.

How do we achieve this 'believability factor'? By inspecting, at first or second hand, the prototype. Look to see where panel lines are obvious, where there are gaps between panels or mouldings, where the most obvious scratches and paint flaking take place, where the oil leaks are, where there are dirt marks resulting from projections, ie. rivets, and where the engine exhaust 'sooting' occurs. Take note of the degree of gloss—or the opposite—on the surface. See whether the rubber tyres really look black, as they are often portrayed. If you have the opportunity, take a look in the 'office'—you may be surprised how much colour there is on the instrument panel, on associated instruments and the fabric of the seats and linings. Colour

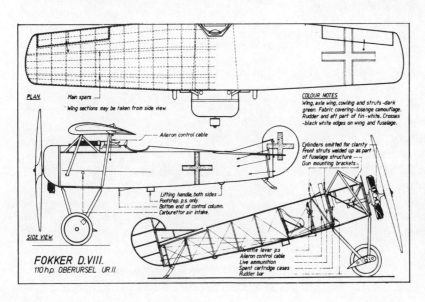

PLAN.
Main spars
Wing sections may be taken from side view.

COLOUR NOTES
Wing, axle wing, cowling and struts -dark green. Fabric covering- losenge camouflage. Rudder and aft part of fin -white. Crosses -black white edges on wing and fuselage.

Aileron control cable

Cylinders omitted for clarity
Front struts welded up as part of fuselage structure
Gun mounting brackets

Lifting handle, both sides
Footstep, p.s. only.
Bottom end of control column.
Carburettor air intake.

SIDE VIEW.

FOKKER D.VIII.
110 h.p. OBERURSEL UR II.

Throttle lever p.s.
Aileron control cable
Live ammunition
Spent cartridge cases
Rudder bar

**Gain as much information as possible on the prototype aircraft and cross refer between drawings, photos and extant aircraft.**

representation is always difficult but there are certain colour references, eg. Methuen, that can be used to compare and check. They may also be used in some of the books dealing with the chosen prototype—if so, try to use the same reference standards yourself.

Flying is a quality of the original which you may be fortunate to witness, or this may be impossible because no example remains in flying condition. Seeing the prototype fly adds two further dimensions to your understanding of the aeroplane. It puts the aeroplane into three dimensions and you can see the 'sit' in the air. You will be able to observe it turning and, if applicable, carrying out aerobatics. Secondly, you will be able to hear the engine (perhaps the 'wind in the wires' too) and propeller, which will help you to reproduce the sound. It is probably true to say that top class modelling standards (static and flying) have reached such a peak that the one area left where *significant* improvements can be made is in scale engine sounds. Where no flying example exists, then we must resort to the written word for information—not a very acceptable alternative but better than nothing. At least the judges of scale contests will probably be in the dark, too!

Millions of words have been written about the 'history of aviation', but it is not all useful to the scale modeller. The books which are the most useful are the reference types such as the Putnam series, the out-of-print series 'Profile', Kookaburra Publications, WW1 Aero, and numerous other series. Treat with caution the 'coffee table' publications which contain beautiful, full-colour illustrations, which look very convincing, but do not necessarily relate to fact!

Monthly magazines, eg. *Aeroplane Monthly*, *Fly Past*, *Air Enthusiast*, *Scale Models* and *Radio Control Scale Aircraft* also contain much useful information and should be indexed for reference purposes. Manufacturers can sometimes be persuaded (via the Public Relations Officer) to supply details of a current or previous aeroplane design. You should be able to find their addresses in a copy of Jane's *All the World's Aircraft* (often available through your local library).

It is impossible to list all the societies, organisations, clubs and other associations who have their interests in aviation. Rest assured however, that someone, somewhere, has some information on your particular model prototype. Researching prototypes can lead to interesting encounters with owners and pilots who can impart that extra bit of knowledge you would never have found in a book. It may even lead you on to an active interest in full-size aircraft—but that is another story.

**Researching prototypes can be informative and exciting – and necessary!**

# Chapter 4
# Aerodynamics

THIS IS the too little or too much chapter! Too little information and you may make mistakes on designing or flying; too much and it may have the non-productive effect of frightening you away from the subject. I will keep it on the simple side and leave the keen aerodynamicists to invest in books such as *Model Aircraft Aerodynamics* by Martin Simons, or his somewhat simpler *Model Flight*, both published by Argus Books. There are also some excellent technical books on full-size aircraft that are also applicable to R/C model flying. Aerodynamics are aerodynamics, and they apply to aeroplanes large and small. The advantage of reading the full-size publications is that they will also describe flight patterns, ie. circuits and landings, basic aerobatics, stalls and spins which we will also be executing with our models. Never be afraid of aerodynamics—you may not understand it all, but what does sink in will be useful information. Our saving grace is that our designing is mainly empirical and our flying mostly by the 'seat of our pants'; however, that doesn't mean that a little extra knowledge couldn't allow us to build a better flying model—or save us from an accident.

There is one essential difference between scale models and the non-scale versions (sports, aerobatic, pylon racing, competition designs etc.). With scale designs, the dimensions, layouts and profiles are all preordained, and they have to be copied as accurately as possible. Non-scale models rely on the designer to establish areas, outlines,

sections and overall dimensions of the model. It might be thought, therefore, that this makes the scale designer's job the easier one. Not so, he must be able to foresee difficulties through following a certain prototype and try to counter the problems within the strict confines of keeping the model an accurate representation. The designer must try to be aware of the potential flight limitations (flight envelope) of the model so that he will be ready for this when the design is flown. Anything that can be done to minimise the adverse flying characteristics of the model (again, without compromising scale excessively), the more pleasant the model will be to fly.

Although most scale models (properly built and not ridiculously heavy) can be made to fly, some of them can be ultra critical regarding the centre of gravity position and with flying limitations—pull too tight a turn with a heavily loaded WW2 fighter and an outside 'flick' is almost certain! Experience and a basic knowledge of aerodynamics will either overcome the problem at the building stage, or prepare you for the dangerous flying conditions to be expected.

So, where are we able to influence aerodynamic design with scale projects? For Class 1 scale designs, we have very little room for manoeuvre; we must adhere strictly to all outlines, areas and dimensions and we must also keep as close to the original aerofoil sections as possible. Incidence angles may be a little more problematic, in that the full-size aircraft is lifting a much greater weight (in proportion) and the incidence

The one we all want to build – and fly – but not the easiest to land.

Bristol 'Boxkite' comes under the 'almost impossible' heading as a flying scale subject.

Wheels had to be moved slightly forwards on the Blackburn 1912 to prevent 'nose-ups'.

setting of the wing may be rather excessive for our model purpose. The loss of 1° of wing incidence may not be noticeable and, fortunately, the tailplane incidence is often adjustable on the prototypes so we can set this to minimise the longitudinal dihedral (angular difference of the wing and tailplane incidence settings) to something more appropriate to the lighter-loaded scale model. A few degrees of engine downthrust may also assist in preventing a 'zooming' climb when it is applied—we often have a greater excess of power (over that required to maintain straight and level flight) than our full-size counterpart.

Good sports-scale weekend flier, the Bristol 'Scout' has ideal proportions for an R/C subject.

One area where we *can* influence the model aerodynamics, and must be totally aware of it, is with the centre of gravity. Almost without exception an R/C model requires a more forward C of G than the full-size prototype (there are good aerodynamic—and piloting—reasons for this). In many instances this will not create any difficulties—it is simply a matter of locating the balance

position further ahead—but it may produce problems with tailwheel, or skid, type aeroplanes, ie. 'taildraggers'. If we take an extreme case, we can ascertain that the Blackburn 1912 monoplane flew with a C of G at about 50% of the wing chord. However, our R/C model will be totally uncontrollable with this positioning and it must be brought forward to, say, 30% of the chord. We now find that this balance point is ahead of or close to the main wheel position and that, statically, the model may balance in a nose down position. We have one further problem with model undercarriages. On the full-size aircraft, nearly all the landing load is taken in the upward direction while, with the model, a larger proportion is a rearward (drag) component caused by the small wheels relative to the fairly rough landing strip (in scale terms). This only adds to the nose overturning moment during landing. An all-too-common sight is to see a 'Spitfire' touch down beautifully only to tip onto its nose a little later in its landing deceleration, when elevator authority reduces and

**Not too steeply away on the climb-out – the 'Spitfire' can have a nasty stall and flick.**

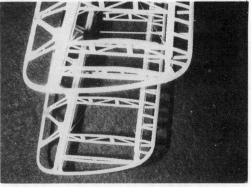

**Careful design and execution of the structure will result in a light airframe and better flying qualities.**

wheel drag takes over. We are left with only two options in these instances (and they are not common to all 'tail-draggers'—some prototypes have the main wheels quite well ahead, another reason for considered prototype selection). We can cheat and move the wheel position further forward, not too easy with retractable undercarriages, or we can accept that a high proportion of the landings are going to finish tail in the air.

With sport scale designs, we have more chance of influencing the aero-dynamic design of the model. Wing aerofoils are a typical area where a modicum of 'artistic licence' (sounds better than cheating) is acceptable. Take a look at some of the aerofoils on early monoplanes and biplanes and you will find they are very slim indeed—the strength of the wing came from the 'ladder' type cross-braced structure and the bracing wires holding the wings in position to the fuselage (the bracing being between top and lower wing panels, for biplanes, or to pylons or the undercarriage structure in the case of monoplanes). Actual wing structures were strong enough for the prototypes where the speed range was minimal and few additional stresses were likely to be placed on the airframe. We would like a little additional security with our model, where we might accidentally

overstress it during flight, and an easy way to achieve this is by thickening the wing aerofoil and increasing the effective depth of the spars. Incidentally, two interesting anomalies with models are that we do not normally require the cross-bracing of the full-size wing structure, but that our covering does increase the stiffness and strength of the wing structure. In full-size, it is not deemed to add anything to the overall strength of the airframe.

Because of the lower wing loadings, our models do not require the same maximum lift requirements as the full-size aeroplanes (have you ever witnessed a model take a scale equivalent length of runway for take-off, compared to the full-size prototype?). It follows, therefore, that we do not need the lift inducers used in modern aircraft to

**Slots, flaps and airbrakes are more effective on large scale models.**

achieve equivalent flight patterns. However, flaps are different. These are not only lift enhancers but also act, with sufficient deflection, in the drag mode—they may be useful to slow the model down on the landing approach allowing us to keep on some power (more control response with prop-wash over elevator and rudder) and to achieve a steeper, scale descent.

The larger the model, the more effective become devices such as leading edge slots (fixed or automatic), drooped leading edges, Fowler flaps (which extend as well as deflect) and other lift-producing or stability-enhancing systems. When you are into the realms of giant scale models, these devices begin to work in a similar manner to those fitted to the prototype aeroplane. This also helps to predict any trim changes brought about by the operation of these systems.

A considerable amount of nonsense has been talked about aerofoil sections for R/C model aircraft. For one thing, with the wing chords we use, and the consequent relatively poor efficiencies, we are not hoping—and do not need—to achieve the lift coefficients of the prototype aerofoils. If we think about open structure wings (as opposed to fully sheeted wing panels), it is obvious that the covering will take the shortest route between the rib stations and that the rib aerofoil is not maintained between ribs. So much for trying to keep

to exact wing profiles! Even with fully sheeted wing panels, we would have to keep excellent accuracies and superb finishes to make efficiency gains with, say, laminar flow. It has been said that, for any chord of three inches or less, we would be just as well to use a flat plate aerofoil section. I can only presume that speed of the aerofoil through the air must also come into the equation, as helicopter rotor blade aerofoils are very critical and they only have chords of one and a half inches or so, but travel at high speeds.

While talking about wing sections, it should be remembered that incidence angles are measured from the fuselage datum (arbitrary, but normally travers-

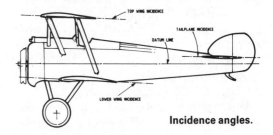

**Incidence angles.**

ing the tailplane or through the engine prop-shaft) to the wing datum line (a straight line taken from the centre of the leading edge and exits through the centre of the trailing edge). The incidence should never be measured to the lower surface of a 'flat bottomed' aerofoil section, eg. Clark Y type. Incidences on biplane wings causes confusion to many designers. Most prototype biplanes use similar incidence settings on the top and lower wing panels, but some have different incidence angles. The aerobatic Pitts biplane, for instance, has positive incidence on the lower wing and negative on the top. I assume that this is to ensure that the top wing stalls before the lower. For many years I have used a setting for my semi-scale biplanes with the lower wing having about ½° less than the top wing. The theory here is that the top wing would be creating more lift and therefore make for a more stable model in normal flight. Stalling these models never produced anything traumatic, and I have come to the conclusion that the settings are not that critical. Keep them as the full-size, with the possible exception of reducing the overall wing/tailplane differential.

Tailplane areas used on full-size aeroplanes are generally adequate for our R/C models, and it is only with some of the smallest area ratios that we might anticipate problems. Areas cannot be considered in isolation. A small tailplane operating over a long moment (distance from wing to tailplane) can provide a more stable (self-correcting) influence than a larger tailplane proportion with a short moment arm. The same considerations apply to fins and rudders, and I can remember feeling distinctly apprehensive about the size of the rudder on an Avro 504 I was making for some television work— it looked ridiculously small at the end of the fuselage. After a couple of flights the concern was entirely forgotten, indeed the 504 had beautifully harmonised controls, whereas the BE2c (with a larger fin and rudder) was defective in directional control. So much for theories and worries!

BE2c (foreground) should, theoretically, have had good flying qualities but lacked directional control.

Centre of Gravity is a term that should be tattoed on the backs of every R/C-model aeroplane enthusiast's hands. The incorrect positioning of the C of G has, with the exception of 'pilot error', contributed to more crashes than any other cause. Although we normally refer to C of G, we should more properly call it the balance point as we, in most cases, are talking about the point on the wings where the model balances longitudinally. Centre of Gravity is the point at which the model is in total equilibrium, ie. in all planes, not just the longitudinal or lateral. Quite simply the positioning of the balance point is critical, as a rearward position will almost certainly end in disaster. A typical scenario with this set-up is for the model to take off before the pilot is prepared, leap upwards with the nose high, corrective action causes an over-response and the model then heads steeply for the ground. From then on, it is a continuous battle with an over-sensitive, unstable model; you may be lucky and put the model down in one piece at the bottom of one of the 'swoops'—or you may be unlucky.

So why do so many modellers risk their creations by attempting to fly them with a rearward balance point? By the nature of things, most scale models, unless great care is taken in building the rear end very light, finish up tail heavy.

Avro 504 proved to have superbly harmonised control surfaces, despite the small rudder area.

This is not too surprising when you consider the mass of engines in the prototypes—in comparison our model engines are much lighter. No one likes to add dead weight to a model (remember, lighter models fly better!) and there is the temptation to ignore the golden rule of 'never fly with a rearward C of G' and prove that you are immune to the laws of physics. You are *not* and you will surely pay the penalty. Conversely, you can often get away with a forward balance point; only if it is excessively forward are you likely to run into troubles, when you might run out of elevator authority as you slow up for the landing (this happened with one of the DH88 Comets where we played excessively safe with the balance point due to the highly tapered wing planform—a stall near the ground would probably be terminal). Having an excessively forward balance point might also bring it very close to the wheel positions on a 'taildragger'. There are a number of formulae for calculating the balance point on various aeroplane configurations and these include the moment arm measurements from the wing to the tailplane. Measurements of the moment arm are taken from the 'mean chord' of the wing and tailplane. Methods of calculating the mean chord and C of G for conventional monoplanes and biplanes are included in the Appendices—ignore them at your peril!

Where we have tapered wing planforms, either from a straight taper or an elliptical wing shape, we must expect problems at the stall. Because of the smaller chord at the tip (and for other reasons) the wing will stall at the tip before it does inboard and this is *not* a desirable effect. When this happens, the wing tip will drop rapidly and that will present all sorts of control difficulties. To reverse the situation, and ensure that the root stalls first, we

Climbing for a stall – and fall – when one engine failed.

can take a variety of actions. The simplest (and used on some full-size designs) is to introduce wash-out, ie. less positive incidence, at the tips. An alternative is to change the wing aerofoil section towards the tip, so that the outboard aerofoil is producing more lift. The third possibility is to fit stall strips to the inboard leading edge or top wing surface to induce the break-up of the airflow before the normal stalling angle would be reached. Again, these are fitted to some prototypes and may be used in scale situations.

Adverse yaw occurs when the down-going aileron creates more drag than it does lift, and yaws the aeroplane in the opposite direction to the required bank. It can happen in a variety of 'planes— full-size and models—but tends to be more prevalent on high wing scale designs. The cure is twofold. One is to introduce differential movement, so that there is considerably more up-going aileron travel than downward deflection. Full-size aircraft overcome the adverse yaw effect by employing Frise type ailerons where the lower edge of the aileron projects into the slipstream as the aileron moves upwards. This introduces additional drag on the wing on the inside of the turn.

Before leaving the subject of aerodynamics we should take a very brief look at the four principal forces acting upon an aeroplane. As previously stated, aerodynamics is a very complex subject and comments here are highly simplified.

### Thrust

In the case of our models, thrust is provided by an internal combustion engine/propeller unit and we have the choice of a diesel engine, two- or four-stroke glo plug or spark ignition motor for the power source. From a flying consideration, there is not a lot of difference between the power sources except that the slower revving engines; ie. *not* the two-stroke glo plug variety, will swing larger diameter propellers and this will suit lighter-loaded, slower-flying models. Do we need to build-in engine sidethrust and downthrust? Prototypes rarely use these devices! For slower-flying models (WW1 biplanes, light aircraft etc.), it does seem worthwhile including both downthrust and side-thrust. Because the wing aerofoils on the slower models tend to be high lift devices, there is a natural tendency for the nose to go skywards as the engine is opened up to full throttle. An injection of downthrust helps to minimise this reaction. Similarly, when the engine is at full power the spiralling slipstream and the reaction to the rotating propeller combine to turn the model to the left. Right engine thrust will help to neutralise this effect. It should be remembered, however, that engine thrust settings can only be a compromise; the requirement actually varies according to the speed and attitude of the model.

### Drag

There is little we can do to affect the amount of drag produced as we are using scale outlines, sections and fairings etc. What we can do is to be aware of the drag factor and understand the influences. High drag aircraft are obviously going to require more powerful engines and, therefore, when the engine quits, the glide is not going to be very efficient. It will need a very steep gliding approach if we are to avoid a stall. Twin-engined models with large radial cowls are another case where drag is an important factor. Have one-engine flame-out and you have the twin dilemmas of no thrust *and* high drag on that side.

### Lift

Unless there are very good reasons against, we will be using a scale wing section and our lift will naturally be related to that aerofoil and the speed of the model. We should, however, be able to learn a little of the characteristics of the aerofoil used, ie. highly cambered section will give a considerable movement of the Centre of Pressure, and that a sharp leading edge will lead to a sharp stall, and vice versa.

### Weight

Just keep it as light as possible commensurate with structural integrity. All decoration and detailing represents non-productive weight—keep it to a minimum.

What if we are modelling an unusual prototype, or there are some non-standard features incorporated? Perhaps we do not know how to calculate the C of G or whether a scale wing section would be advisable?

Start by making a small profile model (from all-sheet balsawood) and test glide that as a simple chuck glider to find the best C of G and, possibly, whether any wash-out is helpful. If you are still determined to continue with the project—and challenge is often the name of the game—build a semi-scale R/C version with the same overall proportions but excluding any of the details. If this performs well, you are on your way!

# Chapter 5
# Putting it on paper

THIS CHAPTER is included on the assumption that you will be designing your own scale model. If your intentions are to build from a plan or a kit, you may still find some of the following information useful, as you may wish to accurately draw aircraft markings or change an aeroplane to a different type or mark.

Many would-be designers are put off the idea because they believe they do not have the design or drafting skills necessary for translating a three-dimensional model aeroplane onto two-dimensional drawings. You do not have to possess great artistic abilities to accomplish the drawing work, and the fact that you are copying an original product makes that side easier. What is important is that you work neatly and methodically and check your work as you go along. There is a natural temptation to rush through the design work so that you can commence the building. Resist this temptation, and put on to the drawing as much information as possible before moving to the workbench. All components should be drawn out (ie. formers, ribs, etc.) and the positions of the engine, radio equipment, linkages, hinges noted, materials specified, methods of assembly worked out and all surface detail included.

Only when you have really thought through all the problem areas, translated the answers to a working drawing, and know exactly how you are going to build the model, should you move away from the drawing board. Like producing a full 'kit of parts' from the drawings (before commencing the actual construction), it will save you a lot of time and frustrations in the long run. One other reason for drawing everything first is, if you are unlucky enough to have to rebuild some part at a later stage, you will need these references. On a commercial basis, you may wish to publish your design in one of the modelling magazines and they will certainly need all the information.

What drawing equipment do you need? In common with workshop tools, the more (within reason), the better. It is possible to design a scale model on the back of a piece of wallpaper using just a straight edge, a pencil and a rubber. It is also the hard way of doing things and unlikely to result in a highly accurate replica. A drawing board and Tee Square, or the modern equivalent, are just about essential equipment, and an adjustable set square is another highly desirable product. You will need a ruler—metric measurements are easier to use than imperial, but you may need to draw in some materials in inches, or fractions of inches. French curves (or better still, railway curves which are longer and more gentle curvature) will help with drawing the subtle curves which most prototypes incorporate. Indeed, careful reproduction of these curves, in outline and section, is vital to create the atmosphere of the full-size aeroplane. You can use a thin flexible strip of hardwood for some curves, and it is possible to purchase flexible curves to follow the curvatures not included in French curve packs.

Investing in a roll of tracing paper

(around 100gsm weight) is well worthwhile. Not only is it a pleasant surface to work on, with pencil or pen, but it is easier to make corrections by erasing mistakes, and it will take a neat crisp line. Perhaps the biggest advantage of all is the potential for obtaining dyeline prints from the finished tracing. Being able to take numerous copies from the original drawing has obvious advantages, as you can use the various printed parts to adhere directly onto the material for cutting out. So, tape the paper to the drawing board and prepare to start.

You will probably have some idea of the size of the model you wish to design, but have not determined an exact scale. A number of factors have to be considered before you can arrive at a logical answer. Assuming that you want to hide the engine—and silencer system—under the scale cowlings of the model, then this will determine the scale, or size, of engine you can use. Roughly sketch out the engine cowl area to the scale you initially contemplate and offer up the engine—or preferably a drawing of the engine—and see whether it will fit. The larger the model, the less

problem you will probably have in fully enclosing the engine and installing a suitable silencer system. For example, Titan spark ignition engines are available in capacities of 23, 38 and 62cc, and the height from the crankshaft centreline to the top of the plug is 140mm for the 23cc motor. The height is rather more than 140mm for the '38' but still only 140mm for the '62', and you have over twice the power!

How do we know whether the power from the engine we propose using will be adequate for the model (when we don't even know what the total weight will be)? Experience is undoubtedly the best guide for these assessments but, if you haven't got personal experience, then 'borrow' from other modellers' experiences. Look at kits and plans of established models and ask around at scale meetings. Try *not* to finish up with marginal engine power—excess power can be dissipated by fitting extra large (nearer to scale!) propellers or from the simple expedient of throttling back. Lack of a reserve of power can be embarrassing, especially at take-off and climb out.

The Andreasson BA4 is a highly aerobatic biplane and a scale model must be sufficiently powered to reproduce the original's performance.

Say that you decide a scale of 1 to 4.2 is about right for the model. You then have to decide whether to keep to an 'oddball' scale or round it out to one of the recognised scales, in this case, quarter scale. The advantage of choosing an accepted scale is that quite a lot of commercial products (canopies, cowlings, decals, wheels, dummy engine cylinders, turnbuckles, metal fittings, pilots, instruments, etc.) may be available to assist with the building and finishing. Many a scale model has been designed around a specific, commercially-available wheel size!

Availability of commercial accessories may influence the scale of the model – and the subject.

Now you have a scale to work to, plus a scale drawing, you can calculate the conversion factor to multiply the scale drawing to bring it up to the R/C model size. Forget about using scale rules for this purpose, as the electronic calculator will give us the conversions in a split second and accurate to a percentage point. All you have to do is measure one reference on the scale drawing, multiply it on the calculator and then transfer that dimension to the R/C model drawing. There are other means of enlarging drawings. If the conversion factor is not too large, say up to about

three times the original, it may be possible to use a photocopying machine to make the enlargements over a series of smaller increases. Over enlarging will introduce too many distortions and inaccuracies. There are also specialist firms who are capable of producing enlargements, at one pass, with drawings of up to 30in. wide and any length. You should also check these enlargements for any distortions. Proportional dividers offer a quick means of making enlargements of measurements, but they can only be used for small dimensions, are not too accurate and should only be used for less critical areas.

Overhead projectors and slide projectors can also be used to project drawings or photographs onto a tracing paper screen where the outlines can be drawn directly, although freehand, onto the paper. Naturally, you must make sure the projection is absolutely 'square' and that it is to the correct scale. It is possible to photograph a scale drawing, with transparency film, and then process this into slide form so that it can be projected from a standard domestic slide projector. Another 'modern' piece of equipment which can help with tedious drawing work is the computer and printer. If you have a wing with a tapered planform and have the root and tip wing sections drawn, you can programme the computer to draw out the intermediate rib stations.

Reverting to the direct measurement system, your first aim should be to rough out the sheet layout, ie. where the fuselage side and top views are to go, and the wing panel (another advantage of using tracing paper is that we can take a reverse print and, therefore, only have to draw a left hand, or right hand, panel). Having decided where the fuselage is to be positioned (and that the paper is long enough), commence the

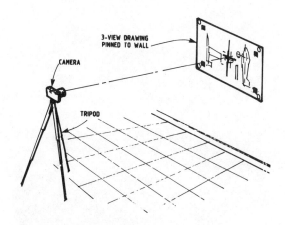

**Photographing scale drawing with a tripod mounted camera.**

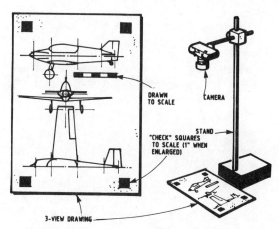

**Taking black and white 'slide' photographs of 3-view drawing.**

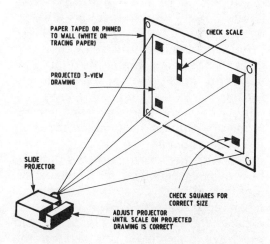

**Projecting the slide for drawing to an increased scale.**

drawing by putting down the datum line on the side view. Scale drawings will often have a datum line shown. This arbitrary line is for reference purposes only (ie. engine thrust line, wing and tailplane incidences etc.), and often runs from the engine propshaft centre-line and parallel to the tailplane incidence. This is not invariable as, for a multi-engined aircraft, for instance, it will not relate to the engine thrust line. If no datum line is indicated on the scale drawing then draw one, approximately centre fuselage at the wing position. Measurements for enlarging will relate to this datum and an equivalent line is drawn on the R/C model plan. Taking measurements along the datum line and above and below the line, transfer the enlarged measurements to your new drawing. Eventually you will have a series of lines and points and you will be able to join these up, in a series of curves or straight lines, to give you a full outline. This is where the extra drawing instruments (including compasses for circles) come into their own. The smaller the radius of curvature, the more dimensions you will have to take to achieve the correct shape; photocopy enlargement of small specific and complicated areas is certainly worth-

while. Alternatively, you can use the squaring method to draw curved areas. Superimpose small squares over the scale drawings and then draw the enlarged squares of your R/C drawing. Following the positions of the curved lines within the squares will give a quite accurate shape.

Follow these methods for the whole of the aeroplane views and sections (making separate drawings of such items as the undercarriage) and you are ready to start 'fleshing in' the structural detail.

# Chapter 6
# Airframe design

RIGHT FROM the very beginning, you will have some fairly definite ideas of the type of construction involved in the model. To a large degree, the structural methods will be determined by the prototype. It would hardly be logical to try to emulate a wooden open structure, covered with fabric, by using glass fibre mouldings. Yes, it has been done, but it seems entirely unsympathetic, to my way of thinking. Wherever possible, the use of identical, or at least similar, materials should be used and, if the prototype used a spruce fuselage frame, wing spars and the wing ribs were built-up from spruce strip, why not use the same methods on the scale replica?

It is with the 'hard' surfaces that we have a wider choice of construction methods. There is a fantastic range of space-age materials with which to experiment. The list is evergrowing and we have only begun to explore the potential of such materials as carbon fibre, boron, Kevlar etc. Don't be afraid to experiment with these materials; find out their strengths and weaknesses and design them into the model airframe. Here is just one small example of how modern materials can overcome problems. The cantilevered undercarriage legs, as used on Cessna aeroplanes, always caused problems with the models—the originals are from high tensile aluminium alloy not available for model use. Either we used the best specification of alloy available, which would 'flatten' on a hard landing, or two pieces of pianowire for the outer edges and faired in between—not a very

DH 'Dragon' model follows full-size constructional methods and materials to a high degree.

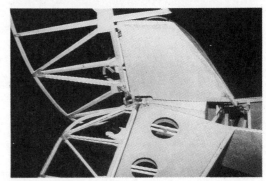

Structural members do not have to be over large for strength.

resilient or robust answer. Now, with the inclusion of carbon fibre tows, we can use a moulded glass reinforced plastic unit which is scale and practical.

Designers of full-size aircraft have different parameters to the R/C modeller, and some are more demanding. Although I have emphasised the importance of keeping weight to a minimum on models, it is even more important with the 'real thing'. In terms of engine size, fuel efficiency, range, take-off distance, climb rate and the all-important pay-load, it is vital that the

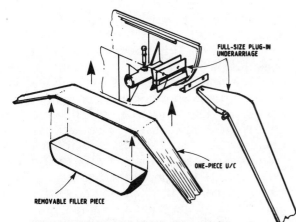

FULL-SIZE PLUG-IN UNDERARRIAGE

ONE-PIECE U/C

REMOVABLE FILLER PIECE

**Full-size cantilever undercarriage can be reproduced with modern GRP processes.**

designer does not waste a pound of weight. In order to achieve these aims, the structure of the airframe has to be carefully designed with the correct stressing of all components. This has been the case right from the earliest days (when the low-powered engines dictated a super efficient/lightweight airframe). We can learn from their works by seeing where the areas of high stress are and where we must similarly reinforce the model airframe.

Early aircraft made great use of bracing and rigging wires and relatively small section wooden members. Forget the stories of aeroplanes made out of bits of wood tied together with string and sealing wax—those designers had to know what they were doing and when failure occurred it was was usually through trying to get a little extra performance from an engine of paltry power, by minimising the airframe weight. Look, for instance, to see where the additional compression struts were positioned in the fuselage and you will find that they are being used to transfer a point load, say from an undercarriage leg, to the main framework. Note how the engine bulkhead support is substantially strengthened by a diagonal brace. See how the centre section strut fixing area and horizontal cross mem-

bers are braced. We should follow the patterns and directions of the wood members, although the wire cross bracing can be dispensed with and plywood gussets fitted to strengthen the joints (and stiffen the framework).

When I first designed scale biplanes, I designed the wing structure so that the panels were fully cantilevered and the bracing wires were purely cosmetic. It was only later when I had to produce a scale model, with virtually scale wing sections, that I resorted to 'working' bracing and rigging lines, only to find that this was the best solution to the problems anyway. It allowed a lighter structure, but the overall strength was greater. The lesson to be learned time and time again is that we can always learn a tremendous amount from the prototype designers. Most of our airframes are considerably over-engineered and heavier than need be. This is understandable, as there is always the fear that we might have a structural failure in the air. So, we work from past experience and maybe add a little extra for insurance. There is an alternative—we can 'sandbag' the airframe when it is completed and before it is flown to check that it is adequately strong for its intended purpose. By varying the load factors, say 3 for non-aerobatic types and 9 for fully fledged aerobatic designs, we can make

**Rigging and structural strengths should reflect the flying usage, ie. aerobatic or non-aerobatic.**

Monocoque fuselages may be moulded, planked or panelled.

realistic checks on the airframe strength. Probably the simple action of carrying out these structural strength tests gives us the confidence to design the structure a little nearer to the stress limits in the first place.

Designing the structure must take into account the transportability of the model, as only the smallest and most compact of models will be left fully rigged. The prototype designers did not have the same problems, in as much as the aeroplanes were not regularly dismantled. However, they had to be erected in the first place and there are normally some 'obvious' places where components are joined together. For example, a biplane will often have the centre section top wing, struts and bracing wires all fitted to the fuselage. The wing panels then bolt to this centre section (and to the fuselage for the

Folding wings on the prototype can be reproduced on the model – eases transport problems.

lower wing panels) by means of brackets and pins. Tailplanes and rudders are frequently one-piece assemblies bolted to the rear fuselage, and the undercarriage invariably bolts onto structural fuselage (or wing) members. Light aircraft, which were often privately owned, sometimes featured folding wings to reduce hangarage charges (normally based on the floor area taken by the aeroplane). Keep to the identical geometry of the prototype—hinge positions, angles, incidence settings—and the wings of your model will fold in precisely the same way. Doing this gives you a model which is easy to transport and delightfully simple and quick to rig.

As aeroplane speeds increased, the older forms of biplanes and wire-rigged monoplanes created too much drag to be efficient. Designers went over to cantilever-winged designs and monocoque fuselages combining low weight with low drag. We have a variety of methods for simulating these structures on our models. Conventional wood materials may still be used with the traditional box structure forming the basis of the fuselage. To this box is added semi-formers, and the whole unit is planked with strip balsa wood and sanded to the smooth contours of the original. Crutch methods may also be used, having a vertical or horizontal crutch, whichever is the most suitable for the design, and building the fuselage in two halves. By having substantial soft balsa wood side crutch members, the fuselage can be built with full formers in one piece. All of these systems rely on a high degree of strip planking, and you should not make the mistake of trying to use fairly wide strips of thin balsa wood for this purpose. It is more satisfactory to use a fairly thick, narrow strip of soft balsa wood and rely on plenty of sanding to bring down the final

**Balsa wood, plywood, foam and GRP mouldings, all used in author's giant Airspeed 'Ambassador'.**

thickness. Using this method and plenty of formers (also from soft balsa wood or foamboard—a useful product for low stressed areas), you will avoid the 'starved horse' effect seen on many scale flying models.

GRP moulded fuselages are very popular these days for metal clad prototypes—the materials used are glass cloth and epoxy or polyester resin. For a 'one-off' model, this system represents a lot of work in producing the male plug' but it is ideal if a number of models are to be built from the same mould. The process of producing GRP mouldings has been written about many times and is thoroughly described, together with other forms of moulding, in the R/C handbook *Moulding and glass fibre techniques*. The vital lesson to learn with any form of moulding is that the finished result *can only* be as

**Working radial engine enhances the scale effect of the 'Corsair'.**

good as the original plug. A mould will faithfully reproduce every minute detail on the original 'plug', even wood grain if that is allowed to show through. Time spent on the original male plug to get the scale accuracy, detail and finish will be well rewarded. A squadron of Spitfires, complete to every rivet and panel line, is much easier to reproduce using moulded fuselages than it would be with traditional wood structures.

Because we have to obtain access to the engine and radio equipment, we cannot have a totally one-piece fuselage moulding, and at least the cowl and the canopy are produced as separate items. Following the actual panel lines of the original will ensure that the fact that cowls or panels are removable is not too obvious.

**Accurate duplication of the fairings – and the 'office' – are essential for believability.**

Wing and tail fairings on modern type aeroplanes are quite difficult to construct and have an authentic appearance. If we take a typical case of a low wing monoplane with generous wing fillets, the model is normally constructed so that the one-piece wing houses onto the fairings. When a continuous flat surface to the top of the wing is used, the fairing is obviously going to stand slightly proud of the wing surface (we may be able to bring the fairing down to a point, but if we also make it then it is likely to curl and distort). To

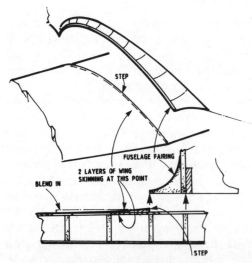

**Forming a fuselage/wing fillet.**

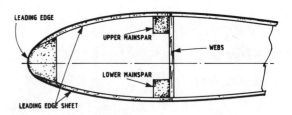

**Typical 'D' box wing construction.**

give a smooth continuous surface between the wing surface and the fairing, it is necessary to use two separate thicknesses of wing skinning on the top surface, thinner in the centre so that the fairing can have more thickness and drop into the recess. Tail to fuselage fairings may best be represented by thin ABS (or similar plastic sheeting) vacuum-formed mouldings. These simulate the beaten aluminium fairings of the prototype and they can include rivet and separate panel detail as well.

Wings can be broadly divided into the open structure, externally braced and the cantilever types, the latter often being fully panelled or sheeted, but not invariably so. There are of course, intermediate varieties where the cantilever is reduced by the use of wing struts from the fuselage to the wing.

As stated previously, the wing fabric covering is not calculated to add to the strength of a full-size wing. It also appears to have another virtue not to be found with model work—it does not adhere to structural components adjacent to the covering. Open structure wings feature near full depth spars where only the top and lower mem-

bers of the built-up rib (not much more than $^3/_{16}$–¼in. deep) extend over the spar, and yet the fabric does not attach itself to the spar upper and lower surfaces between the rib stations. Try that with our model and we are in trouble! This is one reason for increasing the depth of the wing structure slightly, so we can maintain the spar depth but provide a little more gap between the spars and the covering. Keeping to the general design of open structure wings is generally satisfactory, using a sheeted leading edge where that is employed, or the addition of nose riblets. Aim to incorporate a 'D' section leading edge box wherever possible, it makes for a much more rigid wing. We tend to use top and bottom spars rather than, as employed in full-size aeroplanes, the 'I' section full depth spar. By gluing vertical grain webbing between the spars, we virtually come to the same result.

Scale trailing edges can be a troublesome area, the full size timber members can be of quite small dimensions (often resulting in warped

**Exquisite airframe structure of the Proctor Nieuport 28.**

and 'hind leg of a donkey' appearances). It would be helpful if we could increase the thickness of the trailing edge to give more resistance to bending, but this isn't possible and we have to rely on increasing the width to create similar effects. Ironically, the wire trailing edge used on some early aircraft (recognisable by the scalloped effect resulting from the shrinkage of the fabric when it is doped) is quite satisfactory on a model, provided the trailing edges of the ribs are reinforced. You then treat the system as for the full size, and the use of a sewn wing bag is recommended.

When we come to struttery, bracing wires, fittings and so on, there are many ways of achieving this and to give the impression of authenticity. Whatever method is used, it is important first to ascertain the purpose and action of the bracing. Is it there for adjusting the rigging (incidences), does it act as a flying load, ie. under positive G, or as a landing wire when a negative load may be applied? You can roughly calculate the proportion of the total loads being transferred by these bracing wires—it is not too critical, as the wire we use will probably have a high safety factor. Wing interplane struts are always in compression and only need to be located on the wings, not bolted in position. Fully continuous tailplane/fuselage/fin bracing always acts in tension. Understanding the stresses and strains of the prototype will certainly add to your knowledge of how to construct the model.

One area where common modelling practice and full size differ totally is in the use of dihedral braces. In the sense of having additional pieces of plywood glued between two wing panels, the full-size prototypes don't use this system— probably the nearest they get to it is with aircraft such as the 'bent wing' Jodel where the cranked box main spar acts as its own dihedral brace. Wire-braced aeroplanes only have pinned joints where the wing panels attach. There is no continuity in the sense that we use extended wire or wood dowels to assist with a cantilevered effect. With our wire braced models, too, we can safely operate with short stub locators for the wing panels; we only have to consider small shear loads. It is only when we are dealing with cantilevered wings (with detachable wing panels rather than one piece affairs) that we have to incorporate continuity of a structural member. With large models, where detachable wing panels are more convenient, they often take the form of generously sized ali tubes within a tube.

Although foam-cored and veneered wings have become very popular to represent scale wings with 'solid' surfaces, they are not the ideal products for anything but simple scale models. Where retracts, flaps and Frise-type

GRP cowls, balsa wood wing and excellent spray finishing techniques give authenticity to this B-29.

What next?

ailerons are fitted, it is easier to use a built-up, sheeted wing where allowances can be made for including units and fittings during the design stage. Local reinforcement at areas of high stress (where undercarriage legs are bolted for instance) is easier to incorporate with a built-up structure; with foam it is more of a case of hacking away and gluing a ply plate in the hopes that it will spread the load. Size for size, it is also possible to build lighter with balsa wood and plywood and the installation of control linkages and hinges is certainly more straightforward.

Tailsurfaces do not have to carry the high lift loads of the wings, but they do need to be light and warp resistant. Careful selection of the balsa wood is an important factor in maintaining the light weight. Judicious use of lightening holes will also assist in this aim. Early and light aircraft frequently employ tailsurfaces of flat plate section (or nearly so) using a tubular metal or timber construction. For larger scale models we can also use an aluminium tube structure, although brazing aluminium is something of a specialised art; for smaller models it is more normal to use a strip framework with laminated wood for rounded outlines. Where a more substantial aerofoil section is used, normally a symmetrical section,

we can build it on a central sheet core, working on either side with half ribs and sheeted where applicable. Alternatively, where a fully sheeted tailsurface is the aim, we can construct it with a leading edge and trailing edge plus full section ribs—much as we would build a wing.

Whether we build in ailerons as part of the main wing, and cut them away when the structure is removed from the board, or whether we build them as separate items, will depend on the shape and complexity of the ailerons. Building as part of the wing has the advantage of 'continuity' accuracy but, if complex hinges and leading edges are to be fitted, it will probably be better to construct the ailerons as separate items. Flaps come in various types and each present their own structural problems. With the common split flap, the trailing edge tends to be rather thin (not always quite as thin as you might assume—look at the prototype, it may have a reinforcing lip at the rear edge). You will have to use strong materials, such as aluminium, spruce or GRP reinforcement, to keep this edge clean and straight. More unusual flaps, often with extending movements, have to be individually designed and the operation must be 100% reliable. To have a flap extend on one wing and not the other will spell disaster. For this reason, there are obvious advantages in having one centrally-mounted servo operating the flaps via torque rods.

Undercarriages, too, take many forms, ranging from the simple bungee-sprung, common axle types of early aircraft to the multi-wheeled retract versions used on civil airliners and large military aircraft. How accurately we reproduce the undercarriage assemblies will depend on the size of the model and how scale the replica is to be. The smallest scale models do not even

Centre balsa wood core and ribs structure is frequently used for tailsurfaces.

require independent springing—the tyres on the wheels will offer sufficient resilience for a light weight. Even if we do not copy the prototype precisely, in terms of materials and springing methods, a close inspection of the construction, hinging and mode of operation will certainly help us to design an efficient undercarriage. This is particularly true where retracts are involved, as the manner of retracting and extending will have to be faithfully followed in most cases. One area to watch for is wheels retracting into the wings where, on the full size, they rest up against a thin top wing skin when retracted. We are unlikely to have a scale thickness top wing skin and, allied to the difficulty in obtaining wheels sufficiently thin for true scale, it can be difficult to house the wheel and leg fully within a scale wing section.

Either pneumatic or electric actuation is normally used for retract systems (smaller models can have the undercarriage operated directly from a powerful servo). Pneumatics tend to be more positive in operation—providing you remember to pump up the air reservoir—but are more difficult to adjust as far as speed of operation is concerned. It does *not* look very scale when the undercarriage legs snap down in a split second, even if it is a comforting sight to the model pilot.

Scale R/C model aircraft incorporate more metal components than other types—except for helicopters—and we must take on board the skills of the metalworker in addition to those of 'balsa-basher'. Probably, before entering the scale field, we were only conversant with soft soldering; by enlarging our scope to include silver soldering and brazing—plus a modest skill in metal beating and turning—we can tackle many more projects which were impossible before. Metal fittings can be cut and formed from sheet steel, brass or ali, or it is possible to reproduce components by etching processes on nickel or brass. Getting used to working in metal really does open a whole new field of aeromodelling, as it can include airframes as well as components.

Do keep an open mind on new materials and incorporate them in your designs whenever they provide a stronger, lighter or more durable answer compared with the traditional product. One material now being used in space flight vehicles is a composite of carbon fibre outer surfaces with balsa core (the grain running across the surfaces) and this is a fantastically light and strong material.

Two final thoughts on structures. Full-size aircraft designers do not design their 'planes to withstand a crash—nor should we. By all means make it tough enough to cope with a hard landing (we do put our models down rather harder than do the prototype pilots), but you cannot expect a model to survive a real crash unscathed. Trying to incorporate 'crash resistance' normally involves making the structure unnecessarily strong or, in other terms, heavier, which in turn will make it more likely to crash—it will also crash faster and do more damage! BUILD LIGHT, FLY BETTER.

Finally, if you do become uncertain about a particular aspect of design or construction, take another look at the prototype.

# Chapter 7
# Engine options

THE PRINCIPAL function of the engine is, of course, to provide the propellor thrust to gain the air speed, to generate the lift, to keep the model airborne. For scale models there is a secondary function, and this is to simulate the sound of the prototype. When many of the scale modellers, both contest and fun fliers, turned from two-stroke to four-stroke engines everyone agreed that, soundwise, it was certainly a move for the better. From the screaming (at 12,000 rpm plus) sounds of the two-stroke, which certainly assailed the eardrums, we were transferred to the much more pleasant and quieter sounds of the four-stroke motor. Part of the reason for the more acceptable sound was the lower operating speed (and only firing every other stroke). They provide good torque at relatively low rpm, a definite bonus as far as scale models are concerned.

Although there was general agreement that the sounds were a great improvement, I am not sure that anyone actually stopped to think whether they were actually more scale-like. Bear in mind that many of the full-size engines operate between, say, 1,500 and 4,000 rpm, and you will see that even our slower revving engines are going considerably too fast. Indeed, should there be a 'scale sound' and, if so, is this related to the scale of the model, or the speed it flies, or what? Sound for scale models must be a very subjective topic, but we can make some comparisons. A four cylinder horizontally opposed model, four-stroke *is* beginning to sound like a 'Continental', albeit still too

Unusual Farman prototype has unusual engine complement – two Wankel rotaries.

fast (when prop noise becomes almost as important as the exhaust and mechanical noise). Next year we hope to be fitting a genuine scale rotary engine into a Sopwith Dove biplane. It will be interesting to see if it produces the same distinctive note as the rotaries in the Avro 504 and 'Pup' as flown by the Shuttleworth Collection in the UK. Just to give two examples of the subjectivity of engine sounds—the first is a rather silly one. We were filming with WW1 biplanes for a TV series and for this they 'overcrank' the camera speed so that, when it appears on the screen, the models are slowed down. In general, they dub the sounds of engines (taken from real life examples) over the flying sequences. Realising that any 'sound take' would also be slowed down I asked the sound engineer if he had listened to a 'sound take' of the model engine. 'Yes', he said, 'it sounds like a chimpanzee driving a Norton motorcycle through a jungle'! I understood the reference to the Norton, ie. a single cylinder engine plodding away, but why the chimp? He explained that, during the sound take, a bird was singing and, when slowed down, it sounded like an ape calling. So much for sound suggestions!

The second example is purely a subjective opinion. Andreas Geitz has been flying his beautiful, fifteen-foot wing span DC3 for a few seasons now and it was initially powered by two OS 'Gemini' twin cylinder four-stroke engines—it sounded and looked gorgeous. More recently, it was re-engined with Seidel five cylinder radial engines. It flew just as well but, to my ears at

Geared two-stroke used in this Polish 'Morane' sounded reasonably scale-like.

'Empire of the Sun' B-29 model had two working inboard engines and outboard dummies.

Multi cylinder four-stroke engines are now totally practical – if somewhat expensive.

least, it didn't sound as authentic as with the twin cylinder engines. But I'm darned if I know why! Similarly, a very accurate, quarter-scale Rolls Royce Merlin engine when running sounded fantastic, but not like the full-size engine, and it certainly didn't have that Merlin 'crackle' when it was throttled back.

Our choice of engine for small scale models can include diesels or two- or four-stroke glo motors, although I would only consider the diesel for small lightly-loaded, slow-flying models, where the ability to swing a large propeller is a distinct advantage. For smaller models, two-stroke engines may have the advantage of having a greater output for their overall size, allowing them to be fitted into smaller cowlings. Adequate silencing *is* possible for two-stroke engines, it is just a matter or having a large and substantially constructed silencer chamber.

When we get on to the larger capacity engines, the variety opens up again. Geared engines have never found great popularity with scale fliers, although the attributes of swinging large diameter propellers at low speed should have great appeal. Ironically, the rather frenetic sewing machine sound they make (with the engine turning at healthy rpm and plenty of mechanical noise) is not too far divorced from the prototype rotary engines. Belt-driven reducers have also been tried, with limited success, but there should be room for more experiment in this area.

Multi-cylinder, four-stroke engines may be expensive but they are beautiful objects in their own right; they also have the virtues of being very vibration-free in operation and offer good power outputs for a small frontal area, ie. can be cowled fairly easily. As the manufacturers aim to increase outputs from the

**Spark ignition engines have found favour for powering large models – clean, reliable and inexpensive to operate.**

four-stroke engines, so the noise levels increase (the early examples were *very* quiet). We can, however, silence them by fitting a standard expansion chamber silencer. For engines of 20cc capacity and above, there is plenty in favour of using spark ignition engines. These converted chain saw (and similar commercial units) engines are economical to run, extremely reliable in operation and not too expensive. Against them are the higher vibration levels (although not with the twin cylinder versions), a slightly higher risk of fire from the petrol fuel used, and the possibility or interference to the radio equipment. Having operated about ten spark ignition engines of different types, I can honestly say that on only one occasion have I experienced any radio interference caused by the spark ignition system—and then only intermittent. If care is taken with the installation, and the radio kept well away from the engine, it is unlikely that you will suffer any interference. Should it occur, try facing the engine bulkhead with aluminium foil, fit a suppressed plug (or suppressor in the HT lead) and, failing all else, suspect other metal-to-metal noise—or change the radio!

All model engines run hot and need cooling. Some scale installations call for the utmost ingenuity in routing the cooling air to the engine cylinder/s. It may be a tortuous route, but we must get it there somehow! Take the ubiquitous 'Spitfire' for instance. How are we to get cooling air to the engine when the prototype has a liquid cooled engine? We can cheat and have the cylinder head of the model engine just projecting through the cowling, but purists will object to this. A clever alternative is to take the cooling air through the underwing intakes, duct it via the wings and fuselage to the *rear* of the engine and let the heated air exit between the spinner and the front of the fuselage. The exhaust can be made to exit through the scale exhaust stubs. Most vital with engine cooling is to *ensure* that it is routed absolutely to the most important place, ie. the cylinder head. We *must* duct and baffle the incoming cooling air to that position. We must also ensure that the air, now hotter and greater in volume, has a clear, unobstructed, exit to the outside. Hot weather can cause further cooling problems with cowled engines, and a simple tip here is to increase the nitro content of your fuel in these conditions. More nitro means an equivalent power at richer—and cooler—settings. For safety reasons, an extra couple of percent of oil would also not go amiss.

Some glo engines, particularly when inverted, do not take kindly to running for any length of time at slow speed. On opening up the throttle, the fresh charge of fuel will often put the glow out. This can be cured by fitting an on-board glow system (powered by a single cell nicad) connected so that it energises the plug when the engine is at the idle position. Because it is often difficult to get external access to the engine glo plug, we can incorporate the connection of the on-board glo with the normal plug energising connection, in the form or a jack plug or similar socket.

Rarely do the standard commercial

Ensuring that the engine will fit into the cowl area is an essential early check.

Dummy plastic cylinders are available in certain scales for some prototype engines.

expansion chamber, or tuned pipe, silencers fit within the natural confines of the scale cowlings. Fortunately, there are a number of manufacturers making a whole range of remote expansion chambers, exhaust manifold fittings, connecting tubes and pipes etc. The chances are that you will be able to find a suitable range if you search through the catalogues of one of these specialist firms; if not, it is not too difficult to fabricate your own system from brass sheet silver soldered together. Just remember not to make the expansion chamber area, connecting pipes or outlet tubes too small, and to keep the transition between directions as gentle and smooth as possible. Failure to comply with these basics could result in the engine running hot and a loss of power.

Scale cowlings of prototype aircraft using inline engines often have gently curving cowlings emanating from a generously-proportioned spinner. As our model engines have relatively short crankshafts followed by a tall cylinder head (for a single cylinder engine), it is not always easy to hide the engine away. If we can move the cylinder head back, where the cowl is deeper, we have an improved chance to enclose totally the cylinder. We can achieve this aim by using a crankshaft extension. Short extensions may be available from the engine manufacturer and do not cause any operating difficulties. Longer extensions can result in excessive vibration, the more so unless you are extremely careful with regard to balancing the propeller and spinner. Where extremely long extensions are required, possibly with the fitting of a dummy rotary engine or a model of a 'King Cobra', then the extension shaft must be adequately supported at each end. The R/C model boat fraternity has used these methods for many years and can give a lead in sorting out these problems.

Reverse rotation of engines, for pusher applications (there is always a much larger selection of tractor propellers) and for multi-engined installations (so that the engine can be 'handed' to partially counteract propeller torque effects), are not always available from the manufacturers. With engines equipped with reed valve induction there is no problem, as the engine will normally run equally well in both directions. Engines with a bolted-on front crankcase housing can also be modified to operate in the reverse direction by rotating the housing through 90°. For other engines, enquire at the manufacturers to see whether they can supply alternative components, or get yourself an engine expert!

What propellers to use on a particular engine/model combination? There are no simple answers; the instructions supplied with the engine will give you a guide to the size range to suit the engine, but it is really a case of going out and experimenting to find the ideal combination. Do not assume that particular sizes of propellers from different manufacturers will give similar results—they won't. Pitch sizes are only nominal, and propeller shape and aerofoil sections affect the performance considerably. Glass-reinforced propel-

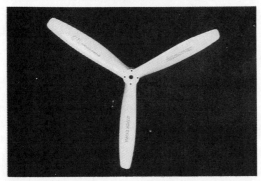

**Propellers and spinners must be perfectly balanced to minimise vibration levels.**

lers have improved in quality and performance over the past few years. although many modellers still prefer to use wooden propellers.

Perhaps the most important aspects of the propeller are that they should be adequately fitted to the engine (multibolted fittings recommended for the largest engines), they track truly, and they should be correctly balanced—this also applies to spinners. There are good prop and spinner balancers on the market—use them!

Bearing in mind the relatively high rpm of our model engines, the propellers we use tend to be smaller than scale. This can cause worries when we have a model with a large diameter cowling and a small propeller—surely we will not get enough thrust with these conditions? Worry not. Even though only an inch or two of the propeller extends past the cowl extremes you will still have the thrust required.

Fuel tank positions can be critical with standard, glo-motor carburettors, and you should aim to keep the tank as close to the engine as possible and with the tank centrelines slightly lower than the carburettor needle valve assembly. Pressure carburettors fitted to the larger spark ignition motors allow you to mount the fuel tank well away from the engine, and it is possible to purchase small fuel pumps—integral with the engine and operated by engine crankcase pressure, or vibration—for standard motors with difficult tank positions. Cleanliness of fuel, fuel tanks and lines is vital if we are to avoid unexpected engine problems. With scale models, in particular, we need absolute reliability of engine operation. Filter fuels at least twice but, if you use an in-line filter (between the fuel tank and carburettor), do ensure it is securely fitted, is cleaned regularly and is airtight. Filters for spark ignition engines need to have a much finer mesh; use an automobile type.

Get to know your engine before it is fitted, and run in your model. Run it on the bench and, if possible, fly it first in a less important sports model before committing it to your scale masterpiece. Never make engine adjustments without very good reason. If you suddenly find that you have to open up the main needle valve by an extra turn or so, the engine is trying to tell you something! Perhaps there is a minor blockage, or the fuel is different (and unsuitable), or the plug is on its way out. Be sure, however, that major adjustment is not caused by a small change in the weather, or a slightly different propeller.

I have made no specific mention here of ducted fan unit installations, as these are a subject on their own. For those contemplating building scale model 'jets' I recommend *Ducted Fans for Model Jets* published by Argus Books— a thorough and fascinating treatise on the subject.

Many modern aircraft are powered by gas turbine engines and the generally accepted method of powering scale models of these prototypes is by using ducted fan systems. High performance engines and fan units are essential for good results and the all important information regarding the design, building and flying of these specialised aircraft is included in this separate publication.

# Chapter 8
# Control systems and linkages

CONSTRUCTION methods of large models and light aircraft are getting to be quite similar; control methods remain poles apart. We are forever condemned to control our scale replicas from afar—even with those getting to almost comparable sizes to the manned replicas. Because we have to remotely control our models (where reaction to situations and positions is inevitably slower and less accurate than with you sitting *in* the aeroplane), we need every advantage there is going. Modern radio equipment is very reliable, but it will only be as good as the way it is installed and the way it is maintained. With scale models, we obviously do not wish to see any part of the R/C equipment and there is a tendency to hide away components— and forget them! Access is vital for all R/C equipment; bear this in mind during the design and construction stages.

If radio equipment is to fail, it is most likely to fail during the first few hours of operation, when any 'weak link' will be discovered. Give the gear a good workout in another model first, and do not be tempted to 'economise' on such items as servos, switches, batteries, extension leads etc. Try to select the frequency you are most likely to be using on a continuing basis. It is not a good idea to be 'digging' into the fuselage to extract the receiver to change the frequency crystal—indeed, in some countries this practice is

**Large model meetings are now a commonplace occurrence.**

**Closed loop control linkages were used on early aircraft and are an ideal system for R/C models.**

banned. Needless to say, the components should be correctly installed and properly protected.

Large models need special precautions, which may be legal requirements or simply common sense. Failsafes, larger batteries, back-up battery systems, special long leads are just some of the items needed to be considered for the larger model. The Argus Books publication *Radio Control Giant Scale Aeroplanes* should help with these considerations.

For scale models—and other R/C models for that matter—we should be looking for control linkages and control surface hinging which offers minimum 'lost' movement (slop!), minimum inertia effects and the most positive control. Although we have our own R/C control linkages, such as wood or glassfibre tube pushrods, plastic 'snakes' etc., there is one linkage system used on full-size aeroplanes which has the potential for the best results. Closed loop linkages have cables from each side of the servo output (or intermediate bellcrank/s) to either side of a control horn on the control surface. Because, with this system, one of the cables is always in the 'pull' mode it is a very positive method; the light weight of the cables (thin stranded metal or nylon covered fishing trace line) keeps inertia to a minimum and, providing the geometry of the linkage and the hinges are sound, the closed loop system is very efficient. With a little forethought and ingenuity, it can be used for most control applications (even for the throttle, although this is less important).

Take, for instance, the aileron control system used on the Avro 504 biplane. The control cable exits the lower fuselages, continues along the underside of the wing to the aileron horn (via a pulley wheel) from the top of the lower aileron a cable connects to the top aileron and, from the upper horn, the cable continues, via another pulley, over wing to the centre section. The opposite side follows a similar route and back to the control column. This route can be recreated on the model, using a suitably powerful aileron servo.

Where cables would be undesirably visible in the fuselage they can be routed, around bends, through small diameter plastic tubing. A small amount of friction is introduced, but not enough

Control cable runs on this Bristol F2B follow the original routes.

to be troublesome. For normal inset ailerons or elevator control linkages, the closed loop system can be taken adjacent to the control surface and terminated in a bell crank (from which is taken a small pushrod and clevis to the horn). Remember that you can also utilise these bell cranks to introduce differential movement and for increasing or reducing the amount of control travel.

I have previously mentioned the advantage of having differential aileron movement (to eliminate, or reduce, adverse yaw), but the throttle is another area where this form of control variation is desirable. We need the most precise carburettor throttle control at the lower speed range of the engine, when we are setting-up for the landing approach for instance. At the higher speed range a variation of a few hundred rpm will not be critical. We can use the servo output connection to obtain this differential.

Modern 'top-of-the-range' radio equipment contains many control variables—including rate control, exponential movements, end limits—as well as other desirable features, such as control coupling, failsafe systems, in-built tachometers, low battery state warnings, etc. We can make use of many of these functions and programs, but remember they can create problems as well as solve them. With a multitude of control variations, it is all too easy to enter the wrong control and that can be fatal. With computerised outfits accepting a number of aircraft programs, one model can be entered to the precise movements and trim requirements and can be 'called up' at any time. Just make sure that all the inputs are exactly what is required and double-check physically with the model before attempting to fly. Such simple devices as servo reversing have brought about the downfall of *many* experienced R/C modellers and the demise of some superb models.

You may have to use your imagination to overcome some of the control linkage routes in scale models. To keep accurately to scale, particularly with modern prototypes where external control horns are noticeably absent, we may have to resort to non-standard forms of actuation. This will frequently entail using shorter control horns (within the depth of the wing structure for instance) than we would normally consider. In these instances, we must be even more vigilant in ensuring there is no lost movement in the form of too large holes in the horns, or sloppy hinges. There is usually more than one answer to a particular problem. Try to select the one that will give the most positive and trouble-free operation. With the larger models, there are trends towards using servos adjacent to the control surfaces and this is much to be

Fowler flaps require a little more thought and ingenuity when transferred into miniature form.

recommended. Servos are now quite small, and all but the smallest have reasonable output thrusts, so it is not difficult to install them in all locations. It reduces the linkage lengths to an absolute minimum, but you must keep a check for possible voltage drop on excessively long leads—also the risk of interference.

Hinges may be of the conventional model types (leaf and pin, or Robart 'horny' type) or may have to be constructed from laminated plastic sheet to follow the principles of the full-size actuation. This is especially true where Frise ailerons and control surfaces with offset hinges are incorporated on the prototype. Whatever the type of hinges and linkages used, the bottom line must be that the surfaces operate smoothly, with a lack of 'slop', are securely fixed (just try pulling them off!) and they move in the right direction!

R/C equipment locations must be planned, efficiently installed and accessible.

# Chapter 9
# Covering finishing and detailing

**B**Y COVERING a model we are trying to achieve a number of aims. For an open structure airframe, we are obviously filling in the holes and establishing, on the wings, a surface which will provide the lift and allow the model to fly. Where soft materials are used in construction, eg. balsa wood, we are also relying on the covering to add protection to the structural airframe and to form a base for the final finish. In all cases, we hope that the covering would add to the overall strength, even if this is only marginal, as may be the case with a doped tissue paper covering.

It follows that, when a prototype has fabric coverings, it should, when being emulated in a smaller scale, also have a type of fabric finish, preferably with the wave to a comparable scale. We should, therefore, be thinking in terms of heat-shrink fabric or nylon and dope covering for scale models of the fabric-covered biplane and monoplanes. Conversely, if we are attempting to recreate a hard 'metallic' surface (or even a fabric surface which has been doped and filled to the extent that it has a fully smooth glossy surface), we might think twice before using a fabric material for covering our model. If we do use it, then we know that we must take the trouble to fill all the open weave to build up to a smooth surface.

Before considering the individual covering and finishing methods, there

**Authenticity involves imitating surfaces and creating weathering effects.**

are a number of 'home-truths' that must be learned. The finished result will only be as good as the preparation on the airframe. You cannot build a rough airframe with the intention of improving the final product at the finishing stages—it just doesn't work that way (short of applying so much filler, primer and paint that the model becomes too heavy to fly at all). You must also realise that the finishing and detailing stages, even when treated with care and consideration, can result in horrendous increases of weight. This is the time you must be at your most 'weight-watching' consciousness.

Heat-shrink fabrics have found tremendous popularity in recent years and it is not difficult to realise why. The ease of application, excellent adhesive and shrinking qualities, availability in many colours and—probably most important of all in a family context—the lack of smell and mess; all contribute to the popularity of these materials. Rarely, however, do you get perfection, and heat-shrink fabrics do have limitations. Unless they are applied and shrunk at the correct temperatures, there is the risk of the covering slackening off when subjected to alternate hot and cold conditions. So use a purpose-made thermometer when applying the covering. A coat of dope, after the covering has been applied, does not go amiss and helps to resist slackening—the last thing we want is for *any* covering to start slackening off *after* we have completed the decoration, added the details and fuel-proofed the model. There are now some excellent silver finish, heat-shrink fabric materials available, in typical inter-war aluminium paint finishes, which do not need additional fuel-proofing (something that caused discolouring with earlier types of silver fabric).

Doped nylon remains an entirely viable option for representing fabric coverings, and some modellers prefer

**Silver finishes are not the easiest to reproduce, but improved silver heat-shrink fabrics are now available – metal should be reproduced with metal!**

this covering system. It does take a little time to become proficient with the application of the nylon (some prefer to attach the nylon dry and others wet) but, once you are familiar with the process, it is very satisfying and results in a tough resilient finish. Brushing the dope, letting the aromas assail your nostrils, picking the dried dope from your fingers is all part of the process—if you don't like it, stick to heat-shrink fabrics. A worrying area for many modellers is trying to get the nylon to adhere to the undercamber of a wing— as the covering is stretched, it naturally tries to pull away from the concave curve of the rib. Some modellers actually stitch the fabric to, or around, the wing ribs (in a scale manner), but this is not really necessary. Before commencing the covering, apply a smear of balsa cement to the already doped and sanded undercamber. Apply the nylon damp and attach the material down the length of the centre by brushing through the dope, so that it reacts with the cement and holds firmly in place. Now work outwards, chordwise, from each side until you have doped down the nylon as far as the leading and trailing edges. Finish by doping through the fabric around the outline of the wing underside and complete the wing panel by adding the top covering (you can use a 'wing bay' as for full-size and follow the same techniques, ie. start by doping through on the centre of the undercamber).

Once the nylon has secured to the rib undersides you can continue to dope the whole panel in the normal way. A final touch with the wing covering which will give authenticity is the addition of rib tapes, with the stitching showing through the tapes. Look at the prototype examples and simulate them with stitching, or PVA glue, and strips of nylon with 'pinked' edges.

Solid finishes, ie. metal or wood panels, of the prototype can be simulated by using equivalent materials, or with a moulded or planked surface sub-divided into panels by the surface finish techniques. Thin plywood or thin aluminium alloy (litho sheet) can be applied to a base airframe in the same sized and shaped panels on the full-size aeroplane, the difference being that we glue the panels in place. The prototype would have rivetted application. We can even use thin card panels, over a fully sheeted structure, to give the impression of a panelled airframe. Where we are using a moulded GRP fuselage, it is naturally sensible to include all of the detail on the original mould.

Assuming that we are starting from a planked or sheeted airframe and will simulate panel lines etc. in the surface finish, we have a number of alternatives for achieving this scale finish. Most traditional is to prepare the airframe by applying a lightweight filler, sanding down, applying more filler, sanding down again and, when really smooth, giving a couple of coats of dope. We are now ready to cover with tissue and this is doped in position, smoothing down over the double curvatures with a soft rag. When complete, further coats of dope and primer are added and the airframe is sanded thoroughly between each coat. Eventually, primer or filler coats are added with the panel lines denoted by masking tape, ie. a slight ridge is built up against the tape. The moral of this process is that we are working *down* to a finish and not up to one. Every time another coat of filler or primer is added, it is sanded away in all parts *except* the low area. By following this process right through to the base colour coats, we will obtain a super finish with a minimum of weight increase.

A tougher alternative to tissue and dope is lightweight glass cloth and resin. There are a number of 'systems'

Cockpits are a delight to the enthusiast scale modeller – plenty of scope for detail.

now available which include the cloth, resin fillers and printers. If it is correctly applied, not being over-generous with the resin and sanding back thoroughly, you will have a really tough skin and good finish with a completely acceptable weight increase. You can then go on and use compatible resin-based paints to decorate the model, without the need for further fuel-proofing.

Heat-shrink films have their place on smaller, sports scale models but are not the best answer where you have to overpaint the covering. The films are ultra shiny, too much so for real scale effect, but they can be toned down by painting with a thinned down matt, or semi-matt, polyurethane clear varnish.

At some point you will have to decide which external details you are going to attach before the final painting and decorating. This is no easy decision, as items such as pilot tubes, ignition switches, guns, windscreens etc. need definitely to look as if they belong to the airframe, but they will certainly get in the way during the sanding-down phases. Probably the best compromise is to wait until you have fully prepared the airframe for the first coat of paint and then add the 'excrescences'. Incidentally, if you don't intend to fully detail the model, then the important items are those that show up silhouette during flight, eg. machine guns, navigation lights, pilot tubes etc. Such items as rivets, walkway scratches and

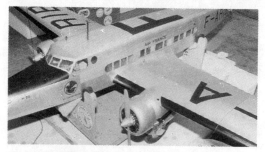

Aluminium litho plate used to represent the original aluminium alloy skinning.

instruments in the cockpit are only going to be visible relatively close up on static exhibition; the flying aspects of scale aeroplanes are still the most important.

Early prototype aircraft, where they were decorated at all, were brush painted; later aircraft had sprayed finishes. We should follow the same procedures. It is possible to brush paint on models of later prototypes, but it gets very difficult to simulate the 'soft' line between camouflaged colours on military aircraft. Spray finishes, on a properly prepared surface, really begin to bring the model to life, the final touch being the dirtying and weathering effects, also best applied with an airbrush. Experience and observation are the best guides to producing a convincing 'used' airframe finish. You should take particular note of the areas which get the most handling, those that show the dirt patterns from the airflow effect in flight and those areas affected by oil and exhaust emissions. I said earlier that no artistic attributes were required in designing the model, but I don't think the same can truly be said when it comes to those final weathering touches—some modellers seem more adept to applying just the right amount, in just the right areas. To help you on your way in this subject I can certainly recommend Ian Peacock's book *Painting and Finishing Models*, published by Argus Books. From there on, it is a matter of experience and experiment.

To a large extent, the more *accurate* detail that is applied, the more believable the model becomes...and yet even that is not entirely true. I have seen scale models which have had scant detailing which, flying a few feet away, *appear* to have everything there. Conversely, some models with every last rivet, panel line and scratch included, have somehow got lost in the sea of detail. Good film and television artists know the answers; they regularly have to give the *impression* of detail with only a few brush strokes. We have to work harder to achieve these results.

How much external detail you fix to the model will ultimately depend on your attitude towards scale modelling. It is not only competition modellers who go overboard with scale detail. Some scale enthusiasts without the slightest vestige of interest in contests will detail to the 'Nth' degree simply out of satisfaction in miniaturising items. What is vitally important (unless you are something of an impressionist genius) is accurately to copy the original, and this usually entails finding out the purpose of the item and how it works. Maybe the detail to be copied is only a blister or a moulding but often it will be part of a mechanical device, and understanding the operation of the device will make it easier to produce in miniature. Perhaps you intend to fit external bombs or disposable auxiliary fuel tanks and have them drop in flight. It is not only important that they release correctly, from a scale release mechanism, but also that they drop to earth in a convincing manner—no-one is going to be awestruck by bombs that float about in the wind. Weight is an all-important factor in these instances—be sure that your model will carry these additional loads without them affecting the flying characteristics to any great extent.

Scale accuracy is important with the external additions and it is equally important to get all the markings, camouflage, lettering and any other painted insignia on the airframe. Do your research thoroughly, crosscheck if possible, because not all references are reliable, and follow them precisely. It is amazing how noticeable can be a very slight difference on, say, the lettering

proportions between the prototype and the model. These differences are all the more noticeable if the model is ever put alongside the prototype; even with the greatest care you will probably notice some transgression. If you have access to the full-size prototype then take a whole series of photographs, trying to keep the subject (whether the complete side view, or only the registration letters) as 'square' to the camera as possible. These photographs can then be studied carefully, and possibly enlarged to full model size, to get the markings correct. And don't forget the underside of the aircraft, an often neglected area (top surfaces can sometimes be viewed from the balcony of a control tower).

As a general point, we might find the reproduction of small painted items, eg. coats of arms, logos, cockpit instruments, badges, etc., rather difficult and time-consuming. By taking a colour print photograph of the area to be copied, and having it enlarged *precisely* to size (take the photograph with a ruler alongside as a reference), we can use it as one would a decal. It is a matter of removing the thin top emulsion (colour) layer of the print, and this can be done by soaking the print in warm water and carefully peeling away the under layers of papers. It might take a bit of experimenting, or using alternative liquids, but it is worth persevering with, as the final result of a thin reproduction glued to the airframe (with white PVA adhesive) can be quite astonishing. It will, of course, need fuel-proofing if it is placed in an area where it is likely to come into contact with fuel.

When the owner of the prototype swears blind that it *is* his 'plane in miniature, then you know you've got it right...until, of course, he adds 'except for that wing tip, I damaged that last week'!

# Chapter 10
# The office and the occupants

**W**ERE I a scale flying judge, I would automatically give zero flying scores to any scale model (with an open cockpit or enclosed cockpit where the occupants could normally be seen) that did not have at least a pilot on view. It is beyond my comprehension that a modeller could spend hundreds of hours making a superb miniature replica of an aeroplane and then fly it—the most important aspect of all—without someone apparently to control the machine. It doesn't happen with the real ones.

In the opposite sense, I am amazed when 'solid plastic' modellers spend a lot of time and very considerable skill in producing a beautifully authentic and detailed cockpit, only to cover it all up when the cockpit mouldings are glued in place—there isn't any chance of seeing the result through the tiny, plastic windscreens. Perhaps self-satisfaction provides the answer here (and is there any other more important satisfaction?) and this also occurs with the R/C scale modeller when he makes a true scale airframe structure (very beautiful in its own right) only to cover it up and for it to be lost from sight for ever. However, back to the office and how we wish to furnish this intriguing area.

I have written in this handbook of the importance of the flying part of scale modelling, but it would be wrong—and impossible—to ignore the static side. If

**For open cockpits and areas where occupants are visible, it is VITAL (for believability) to model them.**

there is a good scale model on the ground with an open cockpit, you can be sure that fellow modellers and interested spectators will be drawn towards that open cockpit. You can almost sense the disappointment if the cockpit/s is bare of any detail, especially if the remainder of the model is well detailed. Logically, if you detail the externals you should also concentrate on the *visible* internals. Anyway, it is really quite a pleasurable occupation, the biggest risk being that you get too carried away by the project.

Cockpits are quite different to any other part of the aeroplane—they even smell different. There is the human touch in these areas which might not be so obvious in other areas; all the components are related to the human scale. For a really convincing cockpit replica, you should be able to imagine yourself sitting in the seat, whether it is the wicker work type of WW1, the aluminium bucket seat of WW2 fighters, or the upholstered style of a modern light aircraft. There is a wide variety of materials and colours that go to make up a fully furnished 'office', and the sizes and shapes of the fittings are considerable. You really do need to absorb the atmosphere of a cockpit. Photographs are not sufficient in themselves and it is very difficult to get a comprehensive series of photographs in an enclosed area. Better for these purposes, if you can get them, are the illustrations from Pilots' Notes on the prototype or which are sometimes published in full-size aviation magazines. These will give the relative positions of all the instruments and equipment, and they extend to the sides and rear of the cockpit as well as the more obvious front panel. You can then

Inspect the 'real thing' if at all possible and notice the natural wear and tear of finishes.

concentrate on the design of the individual items.

Large models really come into their own when we move on to internal detailing. With more room to see inside, and larger individual components 1/3 or 1/4 scale basic flying control panel instruments are quite large), you can go to town on the detailing and the extra wing area will probably cope with the additional weight better. Note how three-dimensional all the cockpit furnishings are; even the instruments have a noticeable 'depth'. Because most of the items in the cockpit are regularly handled, they definitely need to be weathered and, for instance, aluminium panels on the floor will inevitably get scratched. Usually a crowded place, there are a lot of nooks and crannies that are hard to reach and these tend to get a little dusty and

Instruments and controls in the cockpit are three dimensional – not flat.

neglected. Do take the chance of sitting in the cockpit of a full-size aircraft if you have the opportunity; even if it is not the same prototype you are modelling it will give you a much better idea of what it is all about.

Why, oh why, is there such a dearth of scale pilots that look like anything but stuffed dummies... and why do otherwise sane modellers, with exquisite scale models, put a Donald Duck or similar nonsensical figure, in the cockpit? Have you ever seen a duck flying a 'Tiger Moth'? Fortunately, the situation does seem to be improving and no longer are all the model pilots of the 'straight ahead and trust in the Lord' variety, but you will have to search

Instrumentation and a good scale pilot brings the cockpit area to life.

around to find the good ones. It is possible to purchase ready-painted pilots, full torso or bust types, but you must be prepared to pay for the handwork that goes into a well-finished sample.

Most modellers would agree that carving and painting pilot figures is much more difficult than any other part of the aeroplane modelling. It is not so easy to produce a working drawing of the human body, and a replica cannot be constructed in the same way that an airframe can be assembled. It is a matter of carving away from the solid—sculpting—to produce the male plug. From this, you can then make moulds to produce as many as you like (although they will all look the same). By all means have a go at making your own pilot—you may find you have hidden skills—but do your homework first. Get a book out of the library on sculpture, or at least take a series of photographs of a friend (in a helmet and goggles if applicable) and start from correct measurements. The human head is *not* proportioned as many believe.

Painting a face also has its skills and tricks to observe if there is to be life in the finished product. It is easy to reproduce a pilot with goggles or a 'bone dome', but it is more difficult to make him appear animated. The eyes are the part of the head that brings that

Looking for something different? This should exercise your figure modelling skills.

spark of life into an otherwise immovable statue and it is worth taking trouble over these 'windows of the soul'. It is not just the painting of the whites, the iris blue and the pupil black, there is also a reflected highlight on the eyeball that can be denoted by a white dot and a shadow will be cast by the upper eyelid. Shadows are an important part of the painting of the complete figure. Natural light alone will not cast sufficiently 'deep' shadows and these must be enhanced (in the folds and creases of materials etc.) by painting in a darker tone of the colours. Take a look at the art of the military modeller and you will see that his figures have a nice realistic effect.

**We can learn how to paint figures from the modellers of plastic kits.**

Modellers seem to be divided in their attitudes to the detailing of cockpits. To some it is a task to look forward to and for others it is a case of doing just enough to make it look interesting and then ... on to the flying. Back to the subject of pilots, if they allowed me to make the competition rules I would have a separate series of marks for the pilot—that might improve the breed!

**You could almost climb into this cockpit, start the engine and fly away! High level of satisfaction in achieving this standard of modelling.**

# Chapter 11
# Preflight checks and
# test flights

HAVING put a lot of effort into the research, building and finishing of the model, we must not now be tempted to rush the final hurdle. Really thorough checks of the airframe alignments should be made (taking measurements from nose to wing tips, tips to tail and comparing each side) and it is surprising how even small errors can be spotted with a trained human eye. Incidence settings are not so easy to determine by eye or linear measurement, especially if wash-out has been incorporated in the wing. Commercial incidence meters are available and these should be able to cope with wing and tailplane incidences and engine down and side thrust. You may wonder what is the point of taking these measurements at this stage, as it is probably too late to change anything. This may be true, but at least it should give you a warning of what to expect on the first test flight. If there *is a slight*

Use an incidence gauge for checking wing and tail incidences.

difference in the wing incidence (say where the wash-out is incorporated), we can at least compensate in some respect by resetting the aileron neutral position.

You will naturally weigh your model when it is complete. I say 'naturally' because nearly all modellers do, although there is nothing we can do about it at this stage—you cannot add lightness. One thing you can do, and I don't apologise for mentioning it again, is to position the C of G correctly. No matter whether the weight of the model is 50% more than it should be, we must fit additional ballast to the nose if it turns out to be tail heavy. Do not kid yourself that you will be able to handle the 'over-controlling' situation, which a balance point behind that calculated will bring, it may literally be beyond your control! I know that it can be mildly terrifying when the instructions with the kit or plan quote an all up weight of 12lb and your pride and joy ends up at 15½lb. Believe me, it happens quite regularly and I sometimes wonder myself whether the original designers have a different source of balsa wood and paints. Whether the overweight condition will be important depends on the type of model it is, the designed wing loading and the ability of the pilot. A fairly 'hot ship' will be even hotter when the weight is bumped up, but a slow-flying, lightly-loaded design may not

Fast flying models will require relatively small aileron and elevator movements.

have a serious deterioration of flying characteristics. In the terms of the full-size pilots, remember to put a couple of extra knots on for the wife—and one each for the kids—when you make your first landing approach.

If we are scratch designing, what do we allow for control surface movements? Again, it will depend on the type of model; faster-flying aeroplanes tend to need smaller movements than slower types, assuming similar proportions of control surfaces. For example, the amount of rudder area and movement on an SE5a applied to a Pitts Special biplane to the same scale would make it flick roll from here to eternity. However, as an average starting point, think in these terms:

Rudder — up to 30° each way
Ailerons — about 15° up and 8–10° down
Elevator — 15–20° up and down

Slow flying biplanes will need larger control surface movements.

When you can do this with R/C models, I will take up fishing!

Where the transmitter is fitted with rate switches for ailerons and elevators, these should be set at about two thirds movement of the standard setting.

You will, of course, check again for the correct direction of movement of all controls and *not* use the transmitter for flying any other model before the test flying of your new scale design. Engine and radio checks (the final radio check being made with the engine running) should be undertaken, if possible, before the day of flying. If you are going

Check the engine and controls before take-off.

to do these checks on the day of the test flight, be sure not to be talked into rushing through them or, if there is any doubt about the operation of the engine or radio, taking a risk and going ahead with the flying.

First flights should be undertaken on a day when there is not too much wind (although a light, steady wind can be an advantage) and not too many people about. Go for the best flying site that you can find, even if it entails travelling quite a long distance. A site that is flat, with long clear approaches, good ground conditions and an ability to operate with any wind direction, will give you every chance of success. It is another 'unknown' factor eliminated.

Make a written check list of all the vital actions to be taken before flight (including the obvious items of fuelling up, switching on, correct trim settings, etc.) and follow it religiously every time out. You will need a helper in your preparation for flight and during the engine starting. He should also be standing by during the flight to give you reassurance and confirmation of the model's behaviour and attitudes. Brief him on the operation of the auxiliary controls such as the trims, flap lever and settings, undercarriage retract switch. You may have your hands full in trying to keep the model safely in the sky, and having a third hand available to operate

additional functions and trims can be most useful, but you must instruct your colleague precisely and clearly. So, a final check through the engine and radio operation and we are ready to go—once we are sure that no-one else is on the circuit.

Take-off procedures will vary according to whether the model has a tricycle undercarriage or if it is a 'taildragger'. With a trike, assuming you have set the tracking correctly, the model should accelerate in a relatively straight line, into wind, and you only have to make the decision of when to apply some up elevator for lift-off. You may even find that the model will fly itself off the ground as the speed builds up, but you will probably have to introduce a little up elevator to raise the nose wheel and allow the wings to create the lift to climb away. If the model shows no inclination to lift-off even with moderate amounts of elevator applied, and an obvious above stalling speed, you should cast doubts on the ground angle (too nose down) or the relative wing and tailplane incidences.

Taildraggers are, or can be, more of a handful for those first take-offs, until you get used to the particular handling qualities of the model. It is the same with full-size aircraft. Vital actions include heading *directly* into wind and a gentle, but positive, opening of the

A 'second pair of eyes' is a sensible precaution when flying a scale model.

The anxious moment before the first test flight.

Checking engines and having a good take-off surface is even more important with scale twins.

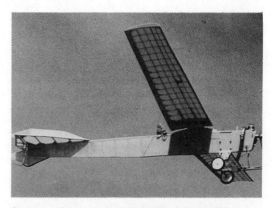

Some models are not suitable for taking off.from anything but the smoothest surface. Hand-launching is an option open for most models.

throttle. If the model starts to swing in one direction during the take-off run, and *small* movements of the rudder do not affect a definite straightening of the direction, then abort the take-off. Try again, this time having the benefit of knowing which way the swing will be, and apply slightly more rudder correction. Continue in this way until you are *anticipating* the swing; the last thing you want is the model leaping into the air in an out of wind direction. Remember that there are a number of forces acting upon the model during take-off, including the precessive, gyro force as the tail rises and the plane of the propeller is moved. Because this force acts at 90° to the direction of the change, it will (with normal anti-clockwise rotation of the propeller) effect a swing to the left. It may be that the take-off swing effects are quite small, but you may also find that you need a permanent right trim on the rudder during take-off and possibly during flight also.

You must always be prepared for the model to become suddenly airborne, before you are ready for this movement. It is often accompanied by a steepish nose-up attitude and, unless you are quick at getting the nose down and the speed built-up, you are risking a stall. Far more models leap precipitately into the air than those that remain resolutely groundborne. If the reason for not becoming airborne is a lack of power, allow the model to reach flying speed then, do not try to coerce the model into the air, it will inevitably become an accident looking for somewhere to happen! A model leaving terra firma rather more quickly than we anticipated may also get into a 'one wing low' state immediately after take-off. Now someone told us that ailerons were used to bring up a low wing to the level position. In normal circumstances this would be true, but not at the slow speed phase immediately after leaving the ground, probably prematurely. The corrective action in this situation, apart from applying down elevator, is to give opposite *rudder*. Using aileron in these conditions may result in more adverse yaw being applied than banking effect of the down going aileron and the real risk of a 'flick' into the ground.

Once safely airborne, and climbing into wind to a reasonable height, our priorities must be to get used to the handling of the model. How responsive are the controls? Over-responsive? Then use the rates' switches to reduce the overall movement. If you have retracts fitted, it is probably as well to leave them in the down position for the first flight. If at all possible, ie. if the model is handling at all reasonably, we want to check the model in the stall, in straight and level and during a turn. Being able to observe when and how the model stalls will give a good indication of how we should fly the down wind turn, approach and touchdown for landing. Carry out a practice circuit to get used to the look and feel of the model in this critical phase and, when it comes to the final touchdown, it is probably safer to try for a 'wheeler' landing, particularly if it is a little windy. Those beautifully-executed, three pointers can wait until later.

What if the unthinkable does happen and, in spite of all the dire warnings and calculations, the model does manage to become airborne with a rearward balance point? You will find that the model is very over-sensitive on control but, worse still, when down elevator is applied, it will continue to dive for the ground even after the elevator has been neutralised. So, you ease on some up elevator and suddenly the model has its nose at an impossibly high angle and running rapidly out of speed. One fact is for sure, there is no point in trying to stay in the air as, once you have got the

Very few prototypes are incapable of being modelled in R/C form and the unique 'Optica' is one that failed to daunt the modeller.

feel of the controls, things are not going to improve. As the fuel is consumed and the balance point moves further back, control will become even more difficult. If your model is equipped with retracts and there is also a grass surface available, put the wheels to the up position and aim to put the model down as softly as possible onto the grass— easier to write about than achieve. You will have to hope that you touch down at the transition between the fugoidal climb and dive. Where tarmac or another hard surface is your only option, then leave the wheels down. In neither instance should you employ flaps, as this is almost certain to make matters worse.

Of course, the chances are that you will not have these problems and that

Only by building and flying a complex scale model – such as this Bloch 200 – can the sense of excitement and satisfaction be fully appreciated.

the model will only require minor trim changes. Your aim now must be to harmonise the controls as far as possible and to familiarise yourself totally with the model. When making trim corrections only carry out one at a time and, when you know the full effect of that correction, you can turn your attention to the next change. Remember that our aim is to fly the model at this magical 'scale speed' and, the more familiar we become with the full flight envelope, the safer we will be when flying at the slower speeds.

With the initial flights, you will probably only see your scale project as another R/C model, and you will be concentrating so much on the flying that it will not register as the model of a particular prototype. As you become more relaxed with the flying, so you will see it in its full glory, be able to carry out low passes without quaking at the

... as the sun sinks slowly in the west.

knees and generally appreciate all the rewards of your efforts.

Whether you visualise yourself sitting in the cockpit, or whether you are quite happy looking from the outside in, enjoy flying the model and the satisfaction it brings. By the way, you did take some photographs of your creation, didn't you? We would love to see one!

# Appendix

## Centre of gravity location

WITH SCALE models we will be looking for pitch stability, whereby the aeroplane will, to some degree, recover itself after being disturbed (by our own hand or wind gusts). Aerobatic scale designs require less inherent stability than, say, an airliner and exactly how stable the model should be will eventually depend on the individual pilot—some modellers prefer highly responsive designs, others are looking for much more docile fliers.

Centre of gravity is directly related to pitch stability and adjusting the balance point will make a model more or less responsive to elevator, ie. move rearward and the model will become, eventually, destabilised. Aerodynamically we are changing the position of the C of G *in relation* to the neutral point (aerodynamic centre) and it is this factor that gives us pitch stability or, if the C of G becomes aft of the neutral point, instability.

For a high proportion of scale models (those with 'normal' layouts and average tail areas and movement arms) a 20–25% average chord centre of gravity position will give reasonable pitch stability and this is a good starting point. Remember, we cannot alter wing or tailplane areas on scale models, so we have to use C of G adjustments for changes of stability (altering incidences will not affect longitudinal *stability*.

To fix the C of G position we must, therefore, be able to position the average chord position and this can be done graphically (for straight tapered wings) as follows.

Transfer the root chord dimensions to either side of the tip chord location—and vice versa—and draw diagonals between those extended points. Where the diagonals cross is the average chord (parallel to the fuselage centre line). Mark the C of G position on this chord line and transfer it to the model. There are, of course, more complicated methods of calculating the desired C of G and reference to aerodynamic books should give the means for finding the balance point for more complex designs. Starting at the 20–25% average chord location will be safe for the majority of scale designs and adjustments can be made according to personal preference and the following guide lines:

### Excessive stability (too forward C of G)

(a) Poor elevator response—needing very large movements.
(b) Large trim changes on elevator (engine on/off).
(c) Unlikely to be able to perform spin— or inconsistent spin entry.
(d) Wing and tailplane incidences not critical.

### Marginal stability (C of G too far rearwards)

(a) Highly responsive elevator control.
(b) Impossible to maintain model in level flight.
(c) High risk of model entering stall (possibly followed by spin).
(d) Trim changes critical—and increasing as fuel is used during flight.

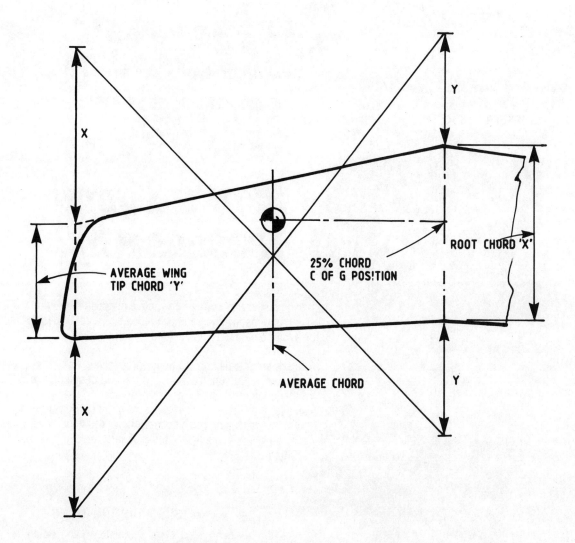

X

Y

AVERAGE WING
TIP CHORD 'Y'

25% CHORD
C OF G POSITION

ROOT CHORD 'X'

AVERAGE CHORD

X

Y

Graphic method of locating position of average chord.